Denmark and National Liberation in Southern Africa

Denmark and National Liberation in Southern Africa

A Flexible Response

Christopher Munthe Morgenstierne

Nordiska Afrikainstitutet, Uppsala 2003

Indexing terms
Foreign relations
National liberation movements
Apartheid
Denmark
Angola
Mozambique
Namibia
South Africa
Zimbabwe

Language checking: Elaine Almén
Cover: Adriaan Honcoop

© The author and Nordiska Afrikainstitutet 2003
ISBN 91-7106-517-2
Printed in Sweden by Elanders Gotab, Stockholm, 2003

Contents

Foreword 9

Preface 11

1. Introduction 13
   Historical setting 14
   The scope of the study 15

2. Out of Anonymity: The Apartheid Appropriation 18
   1960: Consumer boycott and Oliver Tambo's first visit 19
   1962: The Nordic countries in the United Nations:
      'No more Abbyssinia' 21
   1963: Answers to a UN appeal 23
   1964: Denmark's first financial support 27
   1965: Institutionalising Danish support:
      The 'Apartheid Appropriation' 29
   Out of anonymity 30
   Domestic and international Attention 31
   Allocation and distribution: NGOs and the 'Apartheid Committee' 33
   Beneficiaries: Threee broad categories 36
   Volume 1965–1971 38
   Establishing a track for the future 39

3. 'To' or 'Through'? Denmark Supporting National Liberation Movements. . . 41
   1971: The first grant to a national liberation movement 41
   Denmark and its Nordic counterparts 45
   Danish NGO initiatives: 'Afrika-71' 49
   The Social Democrats and the national liberation movements 55
   Liberation movements with human faces: 'But, we knew them' 57
   'Millions to African freedom struggle' 60
   Reactions to Andersen's expansion 63
   Parliamentary debates: 'To' or 'through'? 67
   Dolisie: NGOs favoured over UNESCO 70
   The political nature of Andersen's expansion: Limits for change 75

4. 1974: Political Struggle and Stalemate 77
   Continued growth of the Apartheid Appropriation 77
   New government 79
   A different conclusion 81
   NGOs concerned, but not alarmed 83
   Initiatives for public action 84

Pressure from the right 87
Guldberg suspicious of the Apartheid Appropriation 89
Fighting the minister. 91
Explanations and withdrawal. 92
Political positions 94
Stalemate 96
5. Sanctions: Denmark's Shift from Hesitant to Decisive 98
South Africa back on the agenda 98
Nordic political response 99
Coordinating with the EC. 101
Danish policy on the Nordic Action Programme 102
No restrictions on the coal trade. 103
Public action. 104
Coalition government 1978–79: Cease-fire on sanctions and support. . . . 106
Increasing attention on increasing trade 108
A new government—another new majority 109
Political steps towards Danish sanctions. 111
The Nordic path. 115
Completing Danish sanctions 116
A peculiar parliamentary situation 118

6. Trends and Conclusions 120
Main periods 120
Actors. 121
Double nature and flexibility 123

References 126

Appendix 131

Name Index 142

Acronyms

AAM	Anti-Apartheid Movement of Britain
ANC	African National Congress
DANIDA	Danish International Development Assistance
DCA	DanchurchAid. English for FKN
DGS	Danske Gymnasieelevers sammenslutning (Danish High School Students' Association)
DKK	Danish 'kroner'
DSU	Danmarks Socialdemokratiske Ungdom (the Danish Social Democratic Youth Organisation)
DSF	Danske Studerendes Fællesråd (the Danish Student's Council)
DUF	Dansk Ungdoms Fællesråd (the Danish Youth Council)
EAC	East Asian Company
EC/EEC	European Comunity / European Economic Community
EFTA	European Free Trade Association
FFI	Frie Faglige Internationale (Danish for ICFTU)
FKN	Folkekirkens Nødhjælp
FNLA	Frente Nacional de Libertação de Angola
FRELIMO	Frente de Libertação de Moçambique
Ibis	New name for WUS-Denmark
ICFTU	International Confederation of Free Trade Unions (Social Democratic international labour organization, based in Brussels)
IDAF	Internationa Defence and Aid Fund
IF	Internationalt Forum (Independent youth wing of 'FN-forbundet'—Danish UN Association)
IUEF	International University Exchange Fund
KR	Kirkernes Raceprogram (Danish Section of PCR)
LSA	Landskommiteen Sydafrika Aktion (The National Committee for South Africa Action)
LO	Landsorganisationen (Danish TUC)
MS	Mellemfolkeligt Samvirke
MPLA	Movimento Popular de Libertação de Angola
NATO	North American Treaty Organization
NOK	Norwegian 'kroner'
NORAD	Norwegian Agency for Development Cooperation
OEEC	Organization of European Economic Cooperation
OECD	Organization of Economic Cooperation and Development
PAIGC	Partido Africano da Independência da Guiné e Cabo Verde
PCR	Programme to Combat Rascism (The Danish section was KR)

SACC	South African Council of Churches
SACTU	South African Congress of Trade Unions
SAK	Sydafrika Kommite. (Local South Africa committees. Most prominent were SAK-Århus and SAK-Copenhagen)
SEK	Swedish 'kroner'
SIDA	Swedish International Development Authority (now Sida— Swedish International Development Cooperation Agency)
SWAPO	South West Africa People's Organization
TA	Technical Assistance (Denmark's official development assistance. Did not include the independent 'Apartheid Appropriation')
TS	Technical assistance Secretariate—later DANIDA. Section in the Ministry of Foreign Affairs responsible for administrating the TA. In periods under a different Minister than the Minister of Foreign Affairs. Also responsible for administrating the 'Apartheid Appropriation'
TUC	Trades Union Congress
UFF	Ulandshjælp fra Folk til Folk (Development Aid from People to People—DAPP)
UNITA	União Nacional para a Indepêndencia Total de Angola
USD	US Dollars
WAY	World Assembly of Youth
WFTU	World Federation of Trade Unions (Communist oriented international labour organization, based in Prague)
WCC	World Council of Churches
WUS	World University Service
ZANU	Zimbabwe African National Union
ZAPU	Zimbabwe African People's Union

Danish political parties

Centrum-Demokraterne (CD)	Centre Democrats
Danmarks Kommunistiske Parti (DKP)	Communist Party
Fremskridtspartiet (FP)	Progress Party
Konservative Folkeparti (K)	Conservative Party
Kristeligt Folkeparti (KrF)	Christian Democrats
Radikale Venstre (RV)	Social-Liberal Party
Socialdemokratiet (SD)	Social Democratic Party
Socialistisk Folkeparti (SF)	Socialist Peoples Party
Venstre (V)	Liberal Party
Venstresocialisterne (VS)	Left Socialist Party

Foreword

The present study on Denmark is the fourth and last within a wider research project on *National Liberation in Southern Africa: The Role of the Nordic Countries*, hosted at the Nordic Africa Institute in Uppsala, Sweden. Serving until mid-2001 as the project co-ordinator, it gives me great pleasure that the study by Christopher Munthe Morgenstierne brings this Nordic undertaking to its completion.[1] Studies on Denmark, Finland[2], Norway[3] and Sweden[4] are now available. In addition, a companion volume of interviews—mainly with representatives from the Southern African liberation movements—has been published.[5]

Individually and as a group, from the early 1960s the Nordic countries played a prominent role in support of the national liberation struggles waged against colonialism and minority rule in Southern Africa. While the victorious movements of MPLA in Angola (1975), FRELIMO in Mozambique (1975), ZANU and ZAPU in Zimbabwe (1980), SWAPO in Namibia (1990) and ANC in South Africa (1994) were shunned by the West during the Cold War period as 'Communist' or 'terrorist', their legitimate demands for national self-determination and democracy found an echo in the distant North. Often described as 'Soviet-backed', the less dramatic label of 'Nordic-backed' nationalist movements is empirically more accurate, particularly with regard to the non-military aspects of the struggles. This study on Denmark sheds further light on the Nordic involvement in the 'Thirty Years' War' in Southern Africa which started in Angola in February 1961 and ended with the democratic elections in South Africa in April 1994.

Initially inspired by a research proposal by the Harare-based Southern Africa Regional Institute for Policy Studies (SARIPS) on the the history of national liberation in Southern Africa, in mid-1994—shortly after the demise of apartheid in South Africa—the Nordic Africa Institute took the initiative to

---

1. Due to its marginal interaction with Southern Africa, no particular study on Iceland was undertaken. As acknowledged in the texts, Iceland, however, formed an integral part of the Nordic countries' active stand against colonialism and minority rule.
2. Soiri, Iina and Pekka Peltola, 1999, *Finland and National Liberation in Southern Africa*, Nordiska Afrikainstitutet, Uppsala.
3. Eriksen, Tore Linné (ed.), 2000, *Norway and National Liberation in Southern Africa*, Nordiska Afrikainstitutet, Uppsala.
4. Sellström, Tor, 1999, *Sweden and National Liberation in Southern Africa. Volume I: Formation of a Popular Opinion 1950-1970*, Nordiska Afrikainstitutet, Uppsala, and Sellström, Tor, 2002, *Sweden and National Liberation in Southern Africa. Volume II: Solidarity and Assistance 1970-1994*, Nordiska Afrikainstitutet, Uppsala.
5. Sellström, Tor (ed.), 1999, *Liberation in Southern Africa. Regional and Swedish Voices*, Nordiska Afrikainstitutet, Uppsala.

document the particular involvement of the Nordic countries. More comprehensive accounts of this important chapter in contemporary history will be written from within the region itself. As researchers and participants in the countries concerned increasingly embark on this path, it is hoped that the present study on Denmark, and the other studies in the series published by the Nordic Africa Institute, may contribute to a better understanding of the global context of the Southern African national liberation struggles.

Tor Sellström
Pretoria, 11 November 2003

Preface

Not long after the 1994 elections in South Africa, the joint Nordic Africa Institute in Uppsala, with Project Coordinator Tor Sellström as the organiser, took the initiative to establish research in the Nordic countries to document and analyse their involvement in the Southern Africa liberation process. The aim was to investigate how the Nordic countries developed a policy of support, and how this took its individual form in each of the countries.

The Nordic countries were unique in the Western world in their support to individuals, organisations and refugees, struggling to end institutionalised colonialism and racism and alleviate their humanitarian consequences. Nordic support was humanitarian and civilian, and to a large extent given to refugees and to education. Increasingly, it came to involve national liberation movements and financial support to their civilian activities, at a time when these movements were politically and militarily struggling against the regimes in their countries—including the government of Portugal, a NATO military partner of Norway and Denmark.

Danish support developed differently from that of the other Nordic countries. Official support was never given directly to liberation movements. Rather, Danish NGOs were employed to advise on Danish allocations and to distribute these allocations and carry out activities, using their own capacity or through their international networks.

The study seeks to determine the events, rationales, arguments and decisions that led to the various forms of Danish support. Key questions are *how* Danish support was established as a purely humanitarian facility that later developed into supporting also the liberation movements, and how boycott was first considered to be an issue for the individual but eventually became national, official policy. The study seeks to describe *why* support and sanctions developed in the way and at the pace they did. Major factors involved were Danish public awareness of developments in Southern Africa, domestic political debates and mobilisation through NGOs.

This focus on processes of change has been necessary in a field of Danish foreign relations that during the course of the research was recognised as being a very wide as well as a very interesting one. As a new field of research, and with the majority of the sources never having been studied before, this study has an aim to provide a platform for other researchers, journalists and students. Hopefully it will inspire others to investigate the whole issue further—or to consider it in a different perspective.

This research project has been possible only through the commitment of the Danish Ministry of Foreign Affairs, in the form of financial support and privileged access to central documentation on the administration and development of official support, the so-called 'Apartheid Appropriation'. The project has also been very well received by Danish NGOs and has had access to archives and other material documenting their activities. Finally, a number of individuals who themselves took part in events have been interviewed and have patiently contributed with information and a necessary variety of viewpoints.

The research project has been accommodated in Denmark by the Department of History and Social Theory at Roskilde University and by the Centre of African Studies at the University of Copenhagen, with the help of Professors Gunhild Nissen and Holger Bernt Hansen, respectively. The author is most grateful to both institutions and their staff that have provided not only shelter from the rain, but also encouragement, inspiration and good coffee!

Student assistants Karen Reiff, Kristian Sand and Lone Hvid Jensen have participated at different stages of the research and have each provided invaluable contributions. Veteran commentator Knud Vilby, Professor Gunhild Nissen and editor Anne Hege Simonsen have provided fruitful comments on and important editing of the manuscript. Many others have helped with inspiration and advice during the research process and during the writing, sincere gratitude must be expressed to everybody. Needless to mention, however, the author of the study is solely responsible for all possible flaws and mistakes to be found in the text.

Christopher Munthe Morgenstierne
Tølløse, Denmark, 2003

Chapter 1

Introduction

For more than 20 years, Denmark, together with the rest of the Nordic countries, pursued a political strategy based on the notion that sanctions against apartheid South Africa would lead to nowhere if the UN Security Council did not make them mandatory to *all* UN members—in particular South Africa's main business partners, France, Great Britain and the USA. The Nordic group feared that unilateral sanctions would actually undermine the UN's position, and chose other means to help combat apartheid. In 1986, however, Denmark became the first Western country to introduce full political and economic sanctions on South Africa. This followed, as we shall see, a rather remarkable shift in Danish policy towards the oppressive Southern African regimes.

Bilateral financial support, to humanitarian organizations and later also to national liberation movements struggling against apartheid and colonialism in South Africa, Angola, Mozambique, Zimbabwe and Namibia, became the trade mark of Danish and Nordic assistance. The Nordic countries also played a politically and financially active role in establishing and funding UN initiatives to support victims of apartheid.

Overall, the Nordic countries stand apart from other Western countries in this period. To be in contact with, and even to some extent collaborate with, liberation movements engaged in armed struggle against internationally recognised governments of other countries, was not a common position. In diplomatic terms it was close to being engaged in military activity against these governments. The matter is made not less intriguing by the fact that Denmark, as well as Norway, was a member of NATO, the military alliance which included Portugal—the colonial power in Angola and Mozambique.

Even if the Nordic countries had much in common as a group, each country has its own specific history and approach to the struggle against apartheid and colonialism. In Denmark, it should be noted that this support, to a large extent, benefited from a general political consensus against racism. But, as this study will show, the way it was applied was also subject to vigorous political debate. In particular the political role of the Apartheid Appropriation, a special humanitarian budget allocation established in 1964, which was intensely disputed in the 1970s, mainly due to the differing views of the Social Democrats and the Liberals on the role of the national liberation movements in Southern Africa in a cold war context.

In addition, the role of the Danish NGO's will be discussed. Lots of Western countries had active NGOs and solidarity organizations that informed, lobbied and raised funds to support both humanitarian organizations and liberation movements in Southern Africa. In Britain, boycott and solidarity movements were established as early as in the 1950s, and similar movements could be found in Holland and the USA.

What is significant for the role of the NGOs in the Nordic countries were their relations with their governments. Nordic governments were not only receptive to their arguments; they were actively engaged in supporting the struggle.

In Denmark, NGOs also played an important role as channels for official Danish support to humanitarian organizations as well as to national liberation movements. They were in fact invited to do so by the government, which thereby granted them both influence on official policies and financial support for their Southern African counterparts. On the other hand the NGOs were also influenced in the process by government positions and by official administrative requirements.

In this manner the Danish organizations distinguish themselves from the role their counterparts played in other Nordic countries, where government support was applied directly and where the NGO's role was to debate and comment upon the support.

However, when the question of sanctions came in focus in the 1980s, the relationship between Danish NGOs and the Danish government resembled the situation elsewhere in the Western world, with NGOs lobbying the government.

Historical setting

This study forms the Danish part of a joint Nordic study[1] focusing on the unique role of the Nordic countries in the struggle against apartheid, racism and colonialism from the late 1950s to the early 1990s. Its main focus is to document and analyse the events and processes that formed Denmark's policies and support initiatives, both as a Nordic country with specific characteristics, and as a country making its own individual choices.

It should, however, be remembered that outside the Western hemisphere other countries pushed even harder to end apartheid in South Africa, and to make the colonial powers grant independence to their territories. In the 1960s it was particularly the 'non-aligned countries' and the newly independent African states that struggled to increase UN pressure on a South Africa that showed no will for dialogue or compromise. India had raised the issue of apartheid as early as the 1940s, concerned about the large Indian population in South Africa. Socialist countries saw Southern Africa in an East-West context and supported UN initiatives politically. Over the years they also provided substantial support to the liberation movements, not least military aid. In the

---

1. *National Liberation in Southern Africa: The Role of the Nordic Countries*. Research programme initiated and coordinated by the Nordic Africa Institute, Uppsala.

1960s a majority of UN member countries followed the UN General Assembly's requests to cease diplomatic relations with South Africa, and boycott the country. Western countries did not carry out such measures to isolate South Africa, although most countries supported UN measures against Rhodesia after the unilateral declaration of independence from Britain by its white racist regime in 1965, and many only imposed the UN arms embargo against South Africa in 1978. Otherwise, trade, investments and to a large extent diplomatic relations continued until well into the 1980s, when most countries imposed sanctions. Sweden and Denmark were among the first to do so, respectively banning investment and trade.

The Danish policy towards Southern Africa differs not only from that of many other countries, but it also deviates from the general trends in Danish foreign policy after the end of World War II. After the war, Denmark exchanged a neutrality-based policy that had not prevented five years of Nazi occupation, for alliances with the major Western powers. After 1945 Denmark became an integrated part of the Western world: it joined the NATO military alliance in 1949, received financial assistance from the USA under the 'Marshall Plan', and joined the OEEC/OECD, the EFTA and later EC trade alliances.

At the same time, Denmark felt strongly committed to international cooperation, and was among the founding members of the UN in 1945. After World War II, popular hopes were strong that future conflicts could be solved through peaceful means. In a strict political sense it was also in Denmark's interest—not the least as a NATO member—to work against an increasing divide between the Western and the Eastern blocs ('blocification') engulfing more and more aspects of international relations that would result in reduced areas of manoeuvre for a small country. A strong UN, that could handle and solve conflicts, would counter-act this, as would initiatives from non-aligned countries.

The scope of the study

This study has been carried out in the light of Denmark's position in the global political landscape as a Western and a Nordic country—but also as a unique country with its own specific features. It concentrates on aspects of how Denmark, along with the other Nordic countries, took a different path from most other Western countries, and on issues where Denmark differed from its Nordic counterparts. Thus, it will not focus for instance on the establishing of Danish anti-apartheid movements and their campaigns in the early 1960s; this process was stronger and took place at an earlier stage in other countries. Neither will it go into detail about how Denmark joined UN initiatives initiated by other countries such as the sanctions on Rhodesia in 1966 nor the arms boycott on South Africa in 1978.

The centre of the study is Denmark's official financial support to victims of apartheid, and how this support was expanded and came to include national Lberation movements. Other Nordic countries did likewise, in different ways, but as a whole, this policy was exceptional among the Western countries. Also, the study will deal with official trade sanctions, how Denmark developed from a hesitant passive supporter to a leading initiator.

These are issues that underline official national policy, although it should be noted that the intention of the study is not to promote official policy as a subject of principal importance over public involvement. Public and individual involvement in Denmark was prominent throughout the period; it provided the public with information about the conditions in Southern Africa and worked to persuade the international community and Danish authorities to take action. However, this study will put emphasis on the official decision making layers of society because this is where we find the battlefield for initiatives that carried the heaviest political weight, both domestically and internationally.

Popular movements and their initiatives were important, but they were not unique for the Nordic countries, let alone for Denmark. What was unique was the official political outcome of their efforts. In this capacity, the initiatives, actions and considerations of the popular movements will be investigated and analysed.

The study is also concerned with factors and processes leading to change. In times of change, the nature of such factors and their relative influence become increasingly visible. Also, situations of change, and of having to make one's argument heard, lead—or forced—those involved to consider and sharpen their positions.

A major point of departure is the decisions and considerations made by the Ministry of Foreign Affairs. New material is presented; thanks to the privileged access this project has had to confidential and previously unpublished Ministry archives, concerning the allocation and administration of official Danish financial support. In this material we find reflections on conflicting factors, hesitations and reservations put on paper. Some issues may in retrospect seem rather obvious, but to contemporary decision makers and administrators, support to the distant Southern African region was unexplored territory with unknown determinants and conflicting factors to consider.

The study has also had the opportunity to go through records of involved NGOs, such as Ibis (former WUS-Denmark), DanChurchAid, Mellemfolkeligt Samvirke, Namibia-75, Programme to Combat Racism—Denmark (Kirkernes Raceprogram), the National Committee South Africa Action (LSA) and the Copenhagen South Africa Committee (SAKK). Finally, the project has studied the archives of the late Minister of Foreign Affairs, K. B. Andersen, and parts of the Social Democratic Party's 'Committee of Foreign Affairs Issues'.

In addition, some research has been done into Southern African material, to put the impact of Danish policy and the debates concerning it, into perspective.[1] Though this may seem nationally introspective to some, the study wishes to clarify how Danish actions and reactions to events, developments, problems, conflicts and repression in Southern Africa came about. Hopefully, it will also serve as a Danish contribution to the international history of the struggle against racism and colonialism.

This is a new field of research and a lot of the material has never before been analysed. This requires a certain amount of documentation and outlining. Some readers will perhaps regret this and find the study too descriptive. However, to include too much information rather than too little has been a deliberate choice. A modest request is that this may serve as an invitation, or even a provocation, for others to engage in this rich historical field and to supplement this study by producing alternative or conflicting analyses. Such an an initiative will be most welcomed.

---

1. As a supplement to the regional interviews by the joint Nordic project (Tor Sellström: 1999a) the study has interviewed former representatives to the Nordic countries of SWAPO (Ben Amathila) and ANC (Lindiwe Mabuza). In addition, contemporary press clippings from Southern Africa have been studied that comment on significant developments in the Danish policy.

Chapter 2
Out of Anonymity: The Apartheid Appropriation

In 1964/65 Denmark established a special humanitarian budget allocation, nicknamed 'the Apartheid Appropriation' that for 30 years was Denmark's official financial contribution to the struggle for national liberation in Southern Africa. After a number of major campaigns by Danish organizations to boycott products from apartheid South Africa, the government made a first, one-time allocation administered like other international humanitarian support cases.[1] The Apartheid Appropriation was meant 'to end the anonymity' of Danish support in the 1960s, and it succeeded.

Through the Apartheid Appropriation, support soon expanded from small humanitarian grants to South African students in exile, along the lines of UN recommendations, into an annual several million kroner entry in the government's annual budget in the 1970s. In a close relationship with Danish NGOs, it gradually gained political significance, and from 1971 it even provided a channel for almost bi-lateral relations with national liberation movements struggling for independence throughout Southern Africa.[2]

In addition to the Apartheid Appropriation, Denmark fronted political initiatives in the UN, co-ordinated with the other Nordic countries, and, as in other countries, private Danish organizations mobilised and lobbied for support of the Southern African liberation struggles. Yet, it was the official financial support in the form of the Apartheid Appropriation that developed differently from the other countries. And the debates and decisions concerning its establishment and its use highlight the various Danish positions on the conditions in Southern Africa and on possible Danish action. In this chapter we will look at the early beginnings of the Apartheid Appropriation.

---

1 The Ministry filing number for the appropriation and the committee, '6.U.566'—the main source for this study—reflects the origin of the appropriation: Filing group '6' contains war issues, sub-group 'U' stands for 'wounded, prisoners of war, civil victims, the Red Cross'. 566 is the number among those individual cases.

2 The first official title of the appropriation was 'Appropriation to Humanitarian and Educational Aid to Victims of Apartheid through International Organizations'. After a few years it was changed to '...to Oppressed Groups and Peoples in Southern Africa' instead of 'Victims of Apartheid', and in 1972 it was added: '..and through Liberation Movements'. The 'Apartheid Committee'—the body that in collaboration with the Ministry of Foreign Affairs allocated these funds, was first officially named 'The Advisory Committee to the Minister Concerning Support to Victims of Apartheid'. It was an 'advisory committee to the Minister' of individually selected persons 'with insight in conditions in South and Southern Africa', in practice persons involved in Danish NGOs. The appropriation and the committee were soon nicknamed 'the Apartheid Appropriation' ('apartheidbevillingen') and 'the Apartheid Committee' ('apartheidudvalget'), even if they also dealt with racism in Rhodesia and Portuguese colonialism in Angola and Mozambique.

A few weeks after going into exile, ANC president Oliver Tambo spoke at the Social Democratic May Day rally in 1960. Here after the speech with Prime Minister Viggo Kampmann. (Photo: Polfoto)

1960: Consumer boycott and Oliver Tambo's first visit

On March 21 1960, people gathered in the Johannesburg suburb of Sharpeville, to demonstrate peacefully against the pass laws inflicted on the black population by the South African apartheid regime. The South African police opened fire and 69 demonstrators were killed and 186 wounded. In Denmark, as elsewhere, the event became the turning point for public awareness of the political situation in Southern Africa. Big headlines in the international and Danish press made people in Denmark conscious of conditions that were not acceptable to their own dominating humanitarian and political ideals. Irrespective of their political background, the Apartheid society, built on formalised racial differentiation and the power of the security forces, reminded the Danes of the German Nazi occupation of Denmark, only 15 years earlier.

In December 1959 the International Confederation of Free Trade Unions (ICFTU) of Western social democratic trade unions, morally condemned South Africa's racial policy and recommended its members to launch a consumer boycott, in a joint campaign with the British Anti-Apartheid Movement and the ANC. The trade unions in all the Nordic countries met in Stockholm, and on January 20, 1960, they agreed to follow the ICFTU recommendations. On March 30, the Danish Trade Union Confederation (TUC) (Landsorganisationen De Samvirkende Fagforbund—LO) invited its members, along with Danish consumers and importers, to boycott South African products for a period of two months; April and May. On March 31, Jens Otto Krag, the Social Democratic Minister of Foreign Affairs, evoked the Sharpeville massacres and denounced apartheid in Parliament for the first time. He also said that Denmark would support plans for an extraordinary UN assembly on South Africa, should the ongoing negotiations in the UN Security Council not lead to a positive result.[1]

On May 1, Oliver Tambo, the recently exiled Vice President of the ANC, spoke at the Social Democratic workers' First of May rally in Copenhagen. He told his audience that this was the first time he had spoken to a white audience, and he thanked the Danish workers for their support. He compared the apart-

Oliver Tambo speeks to workers at the B&W Shipyard in Copenhagen, 2 May 1960. (Photo: Polfoto)

heid situation to Hitler's Nazi regime and stressed that a trade boycott, targeting South African products, would be the greatest contribution Denmark could
make to supporting the struggle. Tambo did not focus on the strict economic
effects of such a boycott and he did not talk of state sanctions, but emphasized
the political importance of millions of people in the free world individually taking measures to isolate South Africa. The following day Tambo spoke to 3,000
workers at the Burmeister and Wain shipyard, Denmark's largest employer at
the time. He appealed to the workers to support protest actions against South
Africa and expressed his hope to establish contacts with workers' movements
in the West. He had lunch with Prime Minister Viggo Kampmann and met with
the 'Arbejderbevægelsens InformationsCentral', a social democratic body mon-
itoring communist party and union activity in Denmark.[1]

The Danish consumer boycott in April and May was a success, supported
by a substantial part of the Danish population. It placed South Africa in the
centre of the public debate. Tambo's visit coincided with and was confirmed by
a constant flow of news reports from South Africa. Reports of detentions, tor-
ture and arbitrary shootings of protesters by a racist regime, horrified many
Danes and mobilized backing for the consumer boycott. In turn, the boycott
highlighted developments in South Africa.

---

1. *Trade Union Information Bulletin* no 34, March 1960 (LO newsletter). *Aktuelt*, 1 April. *Berlingske Tidende*, 2 April 1960. The UN Security Council when discussing South Africa and Sharpeville and in its Resolution 134 of April 1, unanimously called upon South Africa to 'bring about
racial harmony', as its apartheid policy was seen to endanger international peace and security, if
continued. United Nations, 1994, p. 244–45.
1. *Aktuelt*, 2 and 3 May 1960. Interview with Lindiwe Mabuza, 15 July 1997. Interview with
Kjeld Olesen, 21 August 1997. Tambo's flight was late and he was rushed to the May Day rally
by taxi by the young party official (and later Minister of Foreign Affairs) Kjeld Olesen. Another
taxi from the same company was parked behind the stage to report on how they were makring it
through the city.

ANC President Oliver Tambo meets with Minister of Foreign Affairs Kjeld Olesen in 1980. Olesen was Tambo's host during his first visit to Copenhagen in 1960. (Photo: Polfoto)

The boycott was backed even by major supermarket chains such as 'Irma' and the cooperative 'Brugsen'. However, the Danish trade volume with South Africa was limited in absolute figures and the economic impact of the boycott insignificant. Its main effect was to put apartheid racism on the political agenda in Denmark.[1]

During the campaign, consumer boycotts were considered an instrument for individuals and independent/private organizations, not for the state. The campaign was arranged by the Danish TUC (LO), with the participation of political parties, including the ruling Social Democratic Party, and organizations such as the Danish Youth Council (Dansk Ungdoms Fællesråd—DUF, an umbrella organization for political, sport, scout etc. organizations). Tambo's official host was 'Arbejdernes Fællesorganisation', a coordinating body of the Social Democratic Union and party branches in Copenhagen. The NGO Mellemfolkeligt Samvirke (MS) ran a fund raising campaign to support victims of apartheid through British/South African Christian Action /Treason Trial, later known as the International Defence and Aid Fund (IDAF).[2] DUF called for Denmark to break diplomatic relations with South Africa if the country did not end apartheid, but in 1960 it was not argued that the state should impose sanctions or take unilateral action other than within the UN framework.[3]

1962: The Nordic countries in the United Nations: 'No more Abyssinia'

The Sharpeville massacre was followed by two years of unrest and oppression in South Africa. As a result, the UN General Assembly adopted Resolution

---

1. *Aktuelt,* 1 April and 2–3 May 1960; *Berlingske Tidende,* 2 April and 2 May 1960; *Løn og Virke* nos. 5, 8-10, 1960.
2. Originally established in 1953 by Canon John Collins at St Paul's Cathedral in London, Christian Aid/ Treason Trial supported legal defence for those arrested in South Africa and gave support to their families.
3. DUF *Lederbladet* 19:3 and 19:5, 1960; Kelm-Hansen, 1981.

1761 on November 6, 1962, stating that the South African government was responsible for the situation. It invited UN member states to take measures against the country, including breaking off diplomatic relations and imposing full trade and communications sanctions. A number of countries, mainly in Africa and Asia, responded to this recommendation and isolated South Africa, whereas countries in the West did not. The resolution was passed with 67 votes to 16 and 23 abstaining. The Nordic countries abstained.[1]

Resolution 1761 further requested the UN Security Council to follow up on the recommendations. This resulted in the Security Council establishing the 'Special Committee against Apartheid'. The Committee met for the first time in April 1963 and submitted reports in May and July that documented the build-up of South Africa's army and police forces. It also recommended the Security Council to consider South Africa 'a threat' to international security. Only a Security Council resolution could lead to mandatory measures for all UN member states, according to Chapter VII of the UN Charter.

In response to an appeal from a meeting of African states in May 1963, the Security Council further adopted Resolution 181 on August 7, after a one-week discussion of the South Africa question. The resolution condemned South Africa's apartheid policies and its harsh measures to enforce them. There was some commitment among member countries to take further initiatives against the country (such as the Kennedy administration's unilateral decision in August 1963 to impose a US arms embargo), but Resolution 181 did not make measures mandatory, as the Special Committee had recommended. It called for a stop in arms shipments, but not for comprehensive trade sanctions, although the formal framework to do so had actually existed since 1960. As a consequence of Sharpeville, the Security Council Resolution 134 of that year had introduced the possibility of mandatory international measures, stating that: 'the situation in South Africa, if continued, might endanger international peace and security'.[2] But in 1963, the Security Council could not agree to follow up on this, nor on the General Assembly Resolution 1761 recommendations of 1962, despite the fact that the situation had actually both 'continued' and become aggravated.

The position of Denmark and the other Nordic countries on UN involvement against apartheid was positive, even if they abstained from voting in favour of Resolution 1761. Prior to the 1962 UN session, the Nordic Ministers of Foreign Affairs had agreed on this position in Helsinki on September 12–13, at one of their regular meetings to discuss and coordinate international policy. They argued that even if a majority in the General Assembly favoured sanctions, they would be meaningless as long as they did not involve South Africa's major trading partners, Great Britain, the USA and France. They wanted to

---

1. Thre were several UN reports and resolutions inviting South Africa to abandon apartheid, but Resolution 1761 was the first to list international measures to put pressure on the country. United Nations, 1994.
2. United Nations, 1994, p. 244–45.

counter the risk of developing a situation similar to when the League of
Nations sanctioned fascist Italy after its invasion of Abyssinia in 1935, sanctions that turned out to be ineffective and eventually undermined the League.
For twenty years this was official policy in all the Nordic countries, and well
into the 1980's it was pursued by a majority of the political parties in the Danish Parliament, including the Social Democratic Party.

As reported by the Danish Social Democratic daily 'Aktuelt', the Nordic
governments had had the opportunity to consult Oliver Tambo on this issue
when he visited the Nordic countries for the second time in August 1962,
shortly before the Helsinki meeting.[1]

After visiting Oslo and Stockholm, Tambo was received in Copenhagen by
Prime Minister Viggo Kampmann, Minister of Foreign Affairs and future Prime
Minister Jens Otto Krag, as well as future Minister of Foreign Affairs Per
Hækkerup. The meeting left no doubts about ANC's call for economic sanctions by the international community, yet, ANC seems to have hesitated about
appealing directly to the governments for state measures. In Oslo, Tambo had
addressed the 'Afro-Scandinavian Youth Congress' where 200 Nordic youth
representatives met with over 100 students from African organizations and
nationalist movements. Tambo appealed to the Nordic participants to campaign for economic sanctions, to 'convince the youth to convince their governments and people...'.[2] In Sweden, ANC stressed its request to isolate South
Africa in a direct letter of September 4, 1962. The letter was signed by ANC
President Albert Luthuli and American civil rights leader Martin Luther King
and addressed to the Swedish Minister of Foreign Affairs Östen Undén. He,
however, never responded.[3]

The meetings with Tambo did not convince the Nordic Ministers to impose
government measures to isolate South Africa economically or diplomatically.
As mentioned above, they agreed to abstain from voting in favour of Resolution 1761, and after its adoption by the UN, the Nordic countries did not use it
as a basis for action. In short, the Nordic policy concerning isolation of South
Africa was not to act ahead of the UN, but to follow. Minister of Foreign
Affairs Per Hækkerup later explained that the Nordic common stand was not
only based on the conviction that UN decisions on sanctions would not be
effective unless they were made mandatory by the Security Council. They also
did not consider it appropriate, in accordance with the internal hierarchy of the
UN, to let the General Assembly interfere with Security Council affairs.[4]
Instead of official sanctions, the Nordic countries preferred to start supporting
the victims of apartheid financially.

---

1. *Aktuelt*, 25 August 1962.
2. Tambo's speech in Oslo, quoted in Eriksen (ed.) 2000, p. 21.
3. Letter from Luthuli and King, see Sellström 1999a, p. 184–85. Sellström here also quotes a letter
   from Tambo of September 5 expressing how satisfied he was with his Nordic tour, including his
   reception in Denmark.
4. Hækkerup, 1965, p. 86. *Aktuelt*, 25 April 1963.

1963: Answers to a UN appeal

From March to May 1963, the Danish youth council DUF carried out a second information, boycott and fund raising campaign. The campaign came as a result of discussions and resolutions at the 'World Assembly of Youth' (WAY) meeting in August in Århus, Denmark and the above-mentioned Afro-Scandinavian Youth Congress in Oslo in September 1962. DUF's member organizations represented a wide political spectrum, but its activities were strongly influenced by Social Democratic youth and student organizations, and coordinated with similar activities in the other Scandinavian countries.

DUF mobilised through its many member organizations, addressed the general public through the press and appealed to 51 organizations, including the political parties, the Danish employers' association (Dansk Arbejdsgiverforening—DA) and the TUC (LO). To advise consumers, DUF published lists of the South African products they wanted people to boycott, and although the Danish market was not significant to South Africa, this campaign, like the one in 1960, was important for mobilising and the spreading of information.[1] The fund raising was handled by the NGO umbrella organization South Africa Fund ('Sydafrikafonden'), a Danish branch of the British based International Defence and Aid Fund (IDAF).[2]

The Social Democratic Youth organization DSU (Danmarks Socialdemokratiske Ungdom) translated and published a booklet by the exiled South African activist Abdul Minty, on South African history and the conditions under apartheid. The book invited both 'housewives and governments' to boycott the country. It also included a DSU statement denouncing the apartheid regime as a parallel to the German Nazi regime and—going further than Minty's text—requested the government to not only use diplomatic channels but also introduce sanctions against the country, in accordance with the UN General Assembly Resolution 1761.[3]

Of the 179 members of the Danish Parliament, 100 signed an appeal to 'support DUF's call for the boycott of South African products'. It should be noted that this appeal was aimed at individuals, and it should not be seen as a first step towards official sanctions. The Chairman of the Socialist People's Party (SF), Aksel Larsen, asked Prime Minister Jens Otto Krag in parliament if he would ensure that no government institutions bought South African products. Krag replied negatively, stating that '... the Nordic governments fully agree that... [sanctions]...should only be launched if they are effective and in

---

1. The campaign reached even conservative middle class homes such as the one of this writer, whose parents stopped buying the family's favourite 'KOO' marmalade and started discussing apartheid.
2. *Aktuelt*, 2 March and 2 May 1963; *Politiken*, 2 May 1963; DUF *Lederbladet* nos. 1–4, January to July 1963.
3. Minty, 1963, p. 12 and 18.

M/S Lommaren leaves Copenhagen harbour with its cargo of South African fruit still on board, during the Boycott South Africa campaign, July 1963. The ship had previously been refused access to Århus harbour and was finally unloaded in Sweden, from where the fruit was sent to Denmark by truck and ferry. (Photo: Peer Pedersen/Polfoto)

accordance with international law—otherwise it will only lead to embarrassment, like the action towards Mussolini taken by the League of Nations'.[1]

Dockers in Copenhagen and Århus were the first to try to boycott South African products collectively. From July 1, no South African goods were unloaded in the main harbours of Denmark. When the Swedish steamer 'Lommaren' called at Århus, with 169 tons of South African fruit for the Danish market, it was not allowed to unload. It sailed on to Copenhagen with the same result. It finally had to land its cargo in its home port of Gothenburg, where the fruit was loaded on trucks and transported to Denmark by ferry. The Danish employers' organization DA argued that the dockworkers' action was technically a strike, and the Court of Arbitration agreed. The workers unsuccessfully referred to the situation in South Africa, claiming that they had merely executed a policy that was supported by everybody, including the 100-member majority in parliament. 34 workers from Århus and Copenhagen were individually fined DKK 35, and their trade unions in Copenhagen and Århus were fined respectively DKK 8,000 and DKK 3,000.

Sanctions remained a question confined to the individual sphere, but there was growing public criticism of the Nordic governments not supporting UN Resolution 1761, not imposing any state measures and not breaking diplomatic relations with South Africa. The official policy was criticised from the left but also from within the ranks of the ruling Social Democratic party. Youth and students who had participated in the Århus and Oslo conferences in 1962 and organized the consumers' boycott in 1963 were particularly critical. Former

---

1. *Aktuelt*, 23 May 1963.

Consumer boycott against South Africa: Social
Democratic Youth picketing at a fruit shop, 1964.

International Secretary of the Social Democratic youth and students' organizations (DSU and Frit Forum) Henning Kjeldgaard commented in the Social
Democratic daily *Aktuelt*:

> Denmark has expressed its sympathy with the cause... but our politicians do nothing!...
> The official reason has been that it would damage the status of the UN if a resolution
> could not be carried out, because South Africa's major trading partners will not impose
> sanctions. This does not at all seem trustworthy...we have previously and without prob-
> lems voted for another UN resolution that could not be carried out: On Hungary in
> 1956.[1]

The next day Minister of Foreign Affairs Per Hœkkerup rejected the argument
in a commentary article repeating the Nordic official policy that unilateral
Nordic sanctions would damage the UN.

Meanwhile the situation in South Africa deteriorated. Popular protests
increased, as did mass detentions without trial. Eight highly profiled leaders of
the ANC, among them Nelson Mandela, were accused of 221 acts of sabotage.
These events compelled the Nordic governments to take their policy on South
Africa one step further.

At their regular coordination meeting, in April 1963, the Nordic Foreign
Ministers issued a communiqué that condemned the racial policies of South
Africa. Six months later, in September, they agreed on making a move in the
UN. In a statement at the General Assembly, on 25 September 1963, Danish
Minister of Foreign Affairs, Per Hækkerup, condemned apartheid on behalf of

---

1. *Aktuelt*, 24 and 25 April 1963. In retrospect Kjeldgaard comments: 'In the Social Democratic
network we saw it as our role to put pressure on the government. Then it was up to the Ministers to work out a government policy'. Kjeldgaard, interview, August 1997.

the Nordic countries, and recommended that the UN assisted in developing a peaceful solution for South Africa, while at the same time maintaining the pressure. Hækkerup stated that the white minority needed 'a way out' that would dampen its fear of losing control of the country. The UN should not only provide the 'stick', in the shape of diplomatic and economic pressure, but also a 'carrot' for the white minority, by recommending a positive transformation of the South African society. The initiative led to Security Council Resolution 182 of December 4, 1963, which repeated the call for a non-mandatory arms embargo, and made the Secretary-General establish a UN 'Expert Committee' to research the options for a future South Africa, chaired by Alva Myrdal from Sweden. On December 16, the General Assembly further adopted Resolution no. 1978B which, based on reports from the Special Committee against Apartheid, stated that families of persecuted persons in South Africa were in need of assistance. The resolution asked 'the Secretary-General to seek ways and means through the appropriate international agencies... and invite member states to contribute generously to such relief and assistance'.[1]

1964: Denmark's first financial support

In February 1964, the Danish embassy in Washington wrote to the Danish Ministry of Foreign Affairs in Copenhagen and asked if Denmark had any plans for supporting young South Africans in exile. The embassy had received a request from the Scandinavia Desk in the US State Department stating that: 'the Department would be greatly appreciative if the Danish government could supply information regarding Denmark's efforts... to support South African students in exile.'[2]

In late December 1963, the Danish Ministry administration considered a grant similar to a Norwegian contribution of NOK 250,000 to the Defence and Aid Fund (IDAF). The Ministry found that Norway was acting in accordance with the UN General Assembly resolutions 1881 and 1978B.[3] They requested the South African Government to end the 'Rivonia Trial' against Mandela and the other ANC opposition leaders, and invited member states to provide relief and assistance to families of politically persecuted people in South Africa. The administration anticipated that the matter would soon be raised as a political issue in Denmark as well. This, however, did not happen, neither in the political nor the public sphere. As a result, the Ministry had taken no action before the inquiry from Washington in February started a process that was at first administrative rather than political.

The American request was handled by the Political Department in the Ministry of Foreign Affairs, a Ministerial body that handles international relations

---

1. United Nations, 1994, p. 265, 270.
2. Letter from the US State Department to the Danish Embassy in Washington, 20 February 1964, MFA 6.U.566.
3. Memo, 30 December 1963. MFA 6.U.566. The Norwegian grant was later increased to 500,000. Eriksen (ed.), 2000, p. 36–37.

on a daily basis and is responsible for contacts with the Danish embassies. They discussed the issue with the Ministry's new secretariat for Denmark's technical development assistance to third world countries, the 'Sekretariatet for Teknisk Samarbejde med Udviklingslandene' (Technical Secretariat for Development Assistance, TS, renamed 'Danida' in 1968). On April 9, a reply to the embassy was drafted; clarifying that the Danish government had no plans for supporting education for South Africans in exile, and neither had private organizations such as the Danish 'Anti-Apartheid Committee'. This draft reply was stopped by the Head of Office and given an appendage explaining that 'the matter seems suitable for further considerations. It appears ... that the Norwegian ini-tiative makes sense and is appropriate for us to follow. Shouldn't this issue be discussed at a higher level?'[1]

On April 20, Mandela gave his famous speech at the Rivonia trial, stating that the ANC was fighting for a democracy that would not result in black domination. The speech was reported in the international media and strengthened international support for the ANC cause. April 20 was also the date when the Myrdal 'Expert Committee' presented its report to the UN, suggesting ways to establish a democratic South Africa for all citizens. It recommended a UN educational programme for non-white South Africans and considered possible measures to impose sanctions against South Africa if the country did not take any steps towards dismantling apartheid.

On April 28, a revised reply was sent to the Danish embassy: 'So far no Danish initiatives have been taken to support these students. In the light of the Norwegian initiative we are, however, considering—in the first place within the Political Department—any background and possibilities for Danish contributions in this field'.[2] By the end of June, the Ministry further notified the embassy that the TS was working on the issue and was preparing a proposal to its Board to support South African students in exile through 'an Organization that calls itself International University Exchange Fund (IUEF) of the International Student Conference'.[3]

The Ministry administration was beginning to explore this new field of operations and engaged itself in establishing background information for an official view of the situation. IUEF was one possible partner considered, and eventually became a major channel for Danish and Nordic support until 1979. When the TS-Board held its next meeting on October 14, it allocated the first official Danish funds to victims of apartheid, through IUEF. The amount was DKK 200,000 (approx. USD 25,000), to be used for the education of refugee students.

---

1. Letter from the Ministry to the Danish Embassy in Washington, 9 April 1964. Not sent. MFA 6.U.566.
2. Letter from the Ministry to the Danish Embassy in Washington, 28 April 1964. MFA 6.U.566.
3. Letter from Technical Secretariat to the Danish Embassy in Washington, 27 June 1964. MFA 6.U.566.

1965: Institutionalising Danish support: The 'Apartheid Appropriation'

During 1964, international hopes faded concerning the South African govern-ment's intentions to enter into any kind of dialogue about reform, as suggested by the Myrdal Expert Committee. In June, UN Security Council Resolution 191 unsuccessfully invited South Africa to grant amnesty to political prisoners, including the Rivonia convicts who had been imprisoned on Robben Island, and to give its response to the Expert Committee proposals. Alternatively, a UN educational programme for refugees would be established. Subsequently, in October 1964, the UN Special Committee against Apartheid issued an appeal to all member states to support the victims of apartheid, and specifically recom-mended IDAF, Amnesty International, Joint Committee on the High Commis-sion Territories and World Council of Churches (WCC) to help dependants of detained, imprisoned and executed persons, refugees and other victims.[1]

The Political Department in the Danish Ministry of Foreign Affairs responded by asking the Technical Secretariat for Development Assistance (TS) to consider supporting such activities on a more permanent basis, as the IUEF grant in 1964 had been a one-time donation. The TS considered the possible character and format of such aid, but had to conclude that such a regular arrangement 'would not fall within the definition of 'technical assistance' as stipulated in the Danish Technical Assistance Act, and... TS therefore has to refuse to fund it'. Consequently, a special allocation would have to be made.[2]

As part of some overall considerations of Denmark's international political profile, the Political Department established in a memorandum, on January 21 1965 that Danish support ought to be 'less anonymous' and more consistent from now on. IUEF practice was to pool funds and help students from all Afri-can countries and not only South African refugee students, and this made the Ministry discuss the possible use of more channels. The fact that Norway, Swe-den and Finland had either embarked on similar support, or were intending to do so, was also taken into consideration.[3]

On January 27, the Ministry internally discussed supporting refugee stu-dents through the Danish Refugee Council and contacts were also made with the Danish Youth Council (DUF), one of the organizations that had played a central role in the 1963 consumers' boycott. DUF was a member of and acted as the secretariat for the South Africa Fund ('Sydafrikafonden'), a Danish branch of IDAF, that worked to raise money. When the Ministry learned that Sweden had granted USD 200,000 to victims of apartheid, they asked the Dan-ish embassy in Stockholm to inquire into what purposes, through which chan-nels and where—inside or outside South Africa—the Swedish money would be utilised. By mid-February it was established that Sweden had granted USD

---

1. United Nations, 1994, p. 283–85.
2. Request from Political Department to TS, 8 December 1964. Response from TS, 15 December 1964. MFA 6.U.566.
3. Memo, 21 January 1965. MFA 6.U.566.

100,000 to IDAF and the World Council of Churches (WCC) respectively. The money was to be channelled through Swedish organizations.[1]

In March the Ministry of Foreign Affairs drafted a request to the cabinet's internal committee on financial issues—a ministerial body coordinating fiscal discipline—to go ahead and apply for DKK 500,000 from the Standing Parliamentary Finance Committee (Finansudvalget). The amount was calculated in consideration of the 1964 grant to IUEF of DKK 200,000 and the fact that the total would equal USD 100,000, half the Swedish allocation and more than the Norwegian one of NOK 250,000. In the application it was argued that Denmark, through this separate budget allocation, 'should give its support more directly, in order to avoid anonymity of Denmark's contributions'.[2] On March 16 the Cabinet Committee approved the DKK 250,000 to be granted to a new appropriation in the annual budget, in order 'to provide official support to victims of apartheid, like Norway and Sweden.' The other half of the suggested DKK 500,000 was to be allocated as ordinary development assistance from TS funds—the Danish development assistance allocation—and given as support to the new UN Education and Training programme for South Africans. The UN Programme was considered to fit into the framework of Danish 'technical assistance', and was going to be implemented in countries where Denmark already had bi-lateral relations. For the bureaucracy this 'fifty-fifty' procedure had the convenient side effect that the overall costs were reduced by 50 per cent, as the TS allocation was already part of the existing budget.[3]

Out of anonymity

In June 1965, the Minister of Foreign Affairs took the application for an appropriation of DKK 250,000 to the Parliamentary Finance Committee, referring to the Cabinet decision of March 16. The Minister motivated the application by drawing attention to the UN resolutions from 1963 and 1964, the Norwegian and Swedish grants from 1963 and 1964, the public backing of the issue, and the procedure from the 1964 grant of DKK 200,000 to IUEF.[4] The se four points indicate a typical pattern for how this kind of support would be explained during the next thirty years: 'UN wants us to do this', 'our neighbours do the same thing', 'we have public backing', and 'what we do is a continuation of existing procedures'.

---

1. Internal note, 27 January 1965. Announcement from the Swedish mission to the UN, 28 January 1965. MFA 6.U.566. Announcement from Sweden's UN mission about a $200,000 grant to victims of apartheid, 28 January 1965. Dispatch from embassy in Stockholm on allocation of grant, 19 February 1965. MFA 6.U.566. On IDAF and its role as a channel for international funding, see: Reddy 1986, United Nations Centre against Apartheid, 1978, and: Collins, Southern Africa: Freedom and Peace, Internet reference.
2. Draft request to the cabinet committee for financial issues, 9 March 1965.
3. Note, Political Department P.J.1, 11 February 1965. MFA 6.U.566.
4. Appropriation Application ('aktstykke') No 467 of 1965/66 to the Standing Parliamentary Finance Committee, 21 June 1965 (in some listings dated 11 October). Printed in 'Finansudvalgets Aktstykker'.

Further, the application underlined that it 'seemed natural and desirable that Danish efforts in the UN for the settling of the apartheid issue were backed by Danish financial support to victims of apartheid'. The new appropriation was described as humanitarian, as support 'to victims of the South African government's apartheid policy, mainly intended for the education and training of young South Africans, especially of those in exile'. It was suggested that the funds could be channelled through UNHCR, WCC, IDAF and possibly the Zambian Red Cross. The application was approved on October 21, 1965.

This was the first and, for seven years, the last time the Apartheid Appropriation was discussed directly by members of parliament. Until 1972, when Minister of Foreign Affairs K. B. Andersen expanded the volume and use of the Apartheid Appropriation, the Appropriation was part of Denmark's general humanitarian allocations. In these years, a pattern of how, to whom and through whom the funds would be allocated was established, i.e. the substance and practices of the Ministry administration and of the advisory 'Apartheid Committee', later established to administer the allocation.

Domestic and international attention

The Apartheid Appropriation *did* succeed in making Danish policy 'less anonymous', both domestically and internationally. Its creation was reported and discussed in the Danish press, and the Danish Youth Council (DUF) issued a press release approving the decision. The UN Secretary General also announced his gratitude for the contribution to the UN Education Programme.[1]

IDAF, however, interpreted the Danish decision too positively and in a letter to the Danish embassy in London they thanked Denmark for its contribution of GBP 12,500 (equivalent to the total Danish grant of DKK 250,000). IDAF board member, Gunnar Helander from Sweden, wrote a similar letter to the Ministry in Denmark. IDAF had been informed through DUF about the new Danish allocation, but they got it wrong. Denmark never allocated the whole amount to IDAF. Even if Sweden in January had decided to support IDAF, and the UN 'Special Committee' had recommended the organization in its appeal in October 1964, IDAF was only one of several candidates considered by the Danish Ministry.[2]

The Ministry had taken note of a news article reporting that the Dutch government had decided to support IDAF, and attached the following commentary: 'If the Dutch can support Defence and Aid with NFL 100,000, we shall also have to do something.' But the Ministry also paid attention to a debate in the Dutch parliament about the 'political nature' of IDAF and the involvement of its founder John Collins in the anti-nuclear 'Ban the Bomb' movement, and

1. *Aktuelt*, 18 June 1965. DUF press statement 18 June 1965. Letter 19 July 1965 from UN Secretary-General. MFA 6.U.566.
2. *Berlingske Tidende*, 14 June 1965. Dispatch from letter thanking for GBP 12,500 to Defence and Aid, 23 June 1965. Letter from Helander to MFA 14 October 1964.

whether or not this would stop the Dutch grant. But the Dutch aid was approved and the Danish embassy in The Hague could report wide popular support in Holland for IDAF.[1]

When Collins and Helander understood that no decision had yet been taken about how the new Danish grant would be allocated, IDAF applied for support, targeting prison education and school fees for children of detainees. These IDAF activities all corresponded well with the framework of the Apartheid Appropriation.[2]

The new Danish grant also received attention from another audience where it was meant to 'end anonymity'—the South African public. When the news of the Danish contribution to IDAF was made public on June 16, it followed in the footsteps of the Dutch grant, which had received strong official and public reactions in South Africa. According to South African Minister of Foreign Affairs Hilgard Muller, IDAF paid the legal expenses for convinced communists and murderers attempting to overthrow the lawful South African government. Denmark's decision to follow the Dutch example in contributing to IDAF was on the seven o'clock radio news the same day, and on the front page of the 'Rand Daily Mail' the day after. The Danish community in South Africa protested to the consulates in Johannesburg and Cape Town. They also cabled the Ministry of Foreign Affairs in Copenhagen claiming that to support IDAF, a fund for apartheid opponents in exile, would be considered 'an unwarranted attempt to interfere with the internal affairs of a friendly country'. The Ministry replied that the main purpose of the decision was to support education for exiles and 'that the humanitarian background should be emphasized'.[3]

This is an early indication of the flexible character of the Danish support. It had two faces, one political and the other humanitarian. Technically, what Denmark actually supported in 1965 and the years to come were humanitarian activities: education, aid to the un-supported families of prisoners, legal assistance, and later health, food supplies etc. But the mere providing of such humanitarian aid to opponents of the apartheid system (and allowing them access to rights denied them by apartheid) was per se a political act. Thus, the reactions of the South African public indicate the political impact of the Apart-

---

1. Dispatches from Danish embassy in the Hague 22 June, 9 July and 1 September 1965. In the July one is noted: 'It seems that the Dutch Foreign Ministry has a certain uncertainty as to whether the Fund or its administration is sufficiently convincing in its claim not to have relations with front organizations'. MFA 6.U.566. For more information on IDAF and Collins, see note 1 on p. 21.

2. Application from IDAF /Collins to Danish Ministry of Foreign Affairs, 8 November 1965. MFA 6.U.566. A total of DKK 66 million from the Apartheid Appropriation was granted directly to IDAF over the years; also, a substantial part of the allocations to UN funds went to IDAF. See appendix.

3. Dispatch from the Danish Consul-General in Johannesburg, 17 June 1965. Cable from The Danish Committee 25 June 1965. Reply via the consulate in Cape Town, 2 July 1965. MFA 6.U.566. Later, the Consulate informed the Ministry that the 'Danish Committee' was dominated by junior civil engineers working for a Danish company awaiting a large contract in South Africa.

heid Appropriation. At the same time, the humanitarian form of the support could, when considered appropriate, be used to neutralise the very same political impact, as shown in the Ministry reply to the Danish community in South Africa.

The ANC branch in exile in Tanzania had also noticed the Danish move and asked the Ministry of Foreign Affairs about support possibilities. The Ministry explained that no decision had yet been made on how the funds would be allocated, but that the new appropriation would be distributed bi-laterally—not via the UN. Investigations were made that eventually led to the ANC not receiving any support. In a copy of one such report (without reference) on the ANC and the educational assistance it received, the Ministry underlined sentences stating that:

> ANC... has large numbers of scholarships to the Communist countries... ANC is now led by a group of serious men who are strongly committed to the left. They are training, and if only Communist countries will offer enough student places, sizable cadres of men will tend to agree with their political analysis (some of course will reject it). If the West *is* trying to compete, it has until now lamentably failed in the perfectly respectable activity of offering education to refugees...[1]

ANC had launched its armed struggle against the South African regime in 1961, and for Denmark it was not possible to fully assess the character and intentions of the organization. ANC President Chief Albert Luthuli was a person held in high esteem, not to mention that he was a Nobel Peace Prize laureate in 1961, and Oliver Tambo had made a positive impression during his visits to Copenhagen in 1960 and 1962. On the other hand, the fact that Tambo, Nelson Mandela and the rest of the younger and more radical generation of ANC leaders had launched the armed struggle just a week after Luthuli received his Nobel Prize is not mentioned in the ministerial files. However, Denmark only wanted to support humanitarian activities, not what was termed 'political' organizations or organizations that might be identified as leftist or terrorist. This could disrupt the image of Danish support as strictly humanitarian and would narrow the flexibility to profile support as humanitarian or political, according to the context.

Allocation and distribution: NGOs and the 'Apartheid Committee'

When Minister of Foreign Affairs Per Hækkerup in June 1965 applied to the Finance Committee for the Apartheid Appropriation, he also suggested forming an 'Advisory Committee regarding humanitarian and educational aid to victims of apartheid' to administer it in cooperation with the secretariat for development assistance (TS). The members of the committee—(soon nicknamed 'the Apartheid Committee') were supposed to be representatives from Danish NGOs with knowledge of South Africa, 'a concept similar to an

---

1. Reply to ANC Secretary General, ANC, Dar-es-Salaam, 15 July 1965. Undated news clipping, filed December 1964. MFA 6.U.566.

arrangement established in Norway', and the committee was supposed to allocate the funds to educational and humanitarian activities, along the lines formulated in UN resolutions and appeals.[1]

In November and December the Ministry considered possible candidates for the committee. A list of 19 organizations was put together, all considered to have the relevant background information and contacts in South Africa. Eventually, eight organizations were invited to join the committee.[2]

Sydafrikafonden (The South Africa Fund—a committee working to raise funds for IDAF), the Danish students' council (Danske Studerendes Fællesråd—DSF) and the Danish youth council (DUF) had all played central roles in arranging public activities and campaigns, and they had also developed significant networks, internationally and in South Africa. Together with the Danish Refugee Council (Dansk Flygtningehjælp) they were suggested from the start as possible channels for the appropriation.

Of the remaining 15, three more were invited to the first meeting: 'Anti-Apartheid Kommiteen' (The Anti-Apartheid Committee), Folkekirkens Nødhjælp (DanChurchAid—DCA) and Amnesty International Denmark. The former was associated with the British Anti-Apartheid Movement and was part of the South Africa Fund together with DSF and DUF. DanChurchAid was a church-based relief and aid organization, associated with the World Council of Churches (WCC), founded in 1922. Around 1960 it shifted its focus from Europe and started supporting victims of the conflicts in Congo and Algeria and carried out 'Bread for the World' fund raising campaigns in Denmark. WCC and Amnesty International had been among the organizations recommended by the UN as channels for support to victims of apartheid.[3]

The last candidate to be invited to join the 'Apartheid Committee' was Danmarks Internationale Studenterkomité (DIS—International Students Committee-Denmark), in its capacity of being the Danish representative and secretariat for the World University Service (WUS) based in Geneva. WUS supported education for non-whites through the organization SACHED (South African Committee for Higher Education) in South Africa.

Representatives of the Ministry and the TS were also 'de facto' members of the 'Apartheid Committee', and a TS official—often the Head of Office—chaired Apartheid Committee meetings, usually accompanied by other officials from the TS and the Political Department.[4] TS came to act as the secretariat for

---

1. Appropriation Application ('aktstykke') No 467 of 1965/66 to the Standing Parliamentary Finance Committee, 21 June 1965 (in some listings dated 11 October). Printed in 'Finansudvalgets Aktstykker'.
2. Notes, 24 November, 10 December and 15 December 1965. Memo 15 December 1965. MFA 6.U.566.
3. 'Appeal to Member States by the Special [UN] Committee... ', 26 October 1964. The appeal was a specification of the appeal in the General Assembly Resolution 1978 B of 16 December 1963 to find 'ways and means of providing relief and assistance'. UN 1994, p. 270, 284–85.
4. This was meant to prevent conflicts with other foreign policy initiatives in the field. Also, decisions on allocation. made by the Committee were to be approved by the Political Department.

the 'Apartheid Committee', receiving the applications and researching background information etc. The Committee became a unique mix of a ministerial body (which it was never designed to be in the first documents) and an NGO forum that allocated funds among themselves or to their international associates.

This structure was not the result of a formal decision. It grew from the practice established by the TS. No bylaws were ever formulated to stipulate the duties, mandate or criteria for membership of the Apartheid Committee or the Ministry administration. In the beginning, the Apartheid Committee was supposed to be the administrative body for the Appropriation. The TS, however, took over the administration and established the Committee as 'an advisory committee to the Minister' in memoranda, minutes from meetings etc. This arrangement was never disputed. The TS officials chaired the meetings on the Minister's behalf, summoned the members, formulated the agendas and wrote the minutes. NGO members gave their opinions, made policy proposals and commented upon allocations, on a general level.

The prominent role of the Ministry in defining the practices and framework for the Committee meant that its decisions never left Ministry control. It also prevented potential conflicts inherent in this paradoxical structure: the individual members of the Committee were appointed because of their knowledge of and contacts with movements in Southern Africa, but the NGOs they represented were also the same institutions that applied for funding from the Appropriation. Had it been a more independent body, the Committee would easily have been suspected of merely distributing funds among themselves. This could have led to accusations of misuse. As 'an advisory committee' the ultimate responsibility remained with the Minister.

This set-up secured that the recommendations of the Committee always stayed harmoniously within the framework defined by the Ministry, and subsequently they were nearly always followed. Of course, realities in Southern Africa sometimes changed after funds had been allocated, and this sometimes affected the procedures. Such situations were handled by the Ministry administration, which sought the approval of one or more committee members. The decisions were then confirmed at the next meeting.[1]

Yet, there were frequent uncertainties about and changes in the procedures, mainly during the first years. As an example the 'Apartheid Committee' was during the first period described in minutes etc. as 'representing' the Danish private organizations, a formulation in accordance with Hækkerup's application to the Finance Committee in 1965. Later, when the Apartheid Appropriation and the Committee became a more controversial issue in Danish domestic politics, it was emphasised that its members were personally appointed by the

---

1. One remarkable exception occurred in 1974, as we shall see in Chapter 4, after the Angolan liberation movement FNLA forwarded an application in 1973 for support to a number of health issues.

Minister and were not included as NGO representatives, on the grounds that the Apartheid Committee was an advisory body to the Minister. When NGOs wanted to change what they considered 'their' members, a formal procedure was developed whereby the NGO applied to the Minister, asking for individual X to become a member rather than individual Y, and the Minister appointed that person. The procedure indicates the lack of formal structures. The Ministry more than once had to check with its own previous practice before a new member was appointed.

No Minister ever met with the Apartheid Committee or was directly in contact with it. The Committee communicated with the Minister through notes and memos. The Minister expressed his views through the officials present at the Apartheid Committee meetings.

Beneficiaries: Three broad categories

The Apartheid Committee met for the first time on January 4, 1966, at the Ministry of Foreign Affairs, and was chaired by the TS Head of Office. The meeting discussed the 1965 appropriation application of DKK 250,000 to the Parliamentary Finance Committee, as this was the closest to a founding document for the Committee. Possible suitable activities inside and outside South Africa were discussed for potential support. The Committee assumed the number of South African refugees in exile to be no more than 2,000, and that sufficient international funds were already available to assist them. It recommended that Denmark should rather fund activities inside South Africa, that were experiencing difficulties in finding donors because of international hesitation to assist organizations ruled illegal or unwanted by the South African regime. It was agreed that IDAF played a central role inside South Africa and would be an interesting channel for funding. The World Council of Churches (WCC) channelled parts of their funds through IDAF, and Amnesty International Denmark supported IDAF-Durban. The Apartheid Committee also anticipated that the planned UN 'Trust Fund for South Africa' would probably use IDAF channels.[1]

The representative from the Danish 'Anti-Apartheid Kommiteen', Niels Munk-Plum, stressed that he considered himself a spokesman for 'more militant elements in [...] South Africa'. He knew several exiled politicians and wanted to know if they could be recognised as channels for educational support. The Ministry officials expressed hesitation about supporting political organizations if other and 'more neutral' channels were available. But they would not totally exclude the option.

Apart from strategic demarcations of position, the first meeting predominantly discussed possible methods and channels for assistance, and it provided information to help the evaluation of the various applications the Ministry had

---

1. The UN Trust started its activities in February and IDAF did become a main beneficiary. Minutes, meeting 4 January 1966. MFA 6.U.566.

received. In November 1965 IDAF had sent an application for support of prison education and school fees for children of detainees; IUEF applied on behalf of St Mary's College for refugees in Roma, Lesotho; the Danish Students' Council (DSF) and World University Service International (WUS-I) wanted to support bursaries from the South African Committee for Higher Education (SACHED) in South Africa; the International Refugee Council of Zambia (IRCOZ) applied for support to the resettlement of refugees and transit transport through Zambia; the World Council of Churches applied via DanChurchAid for humanitarian aid projects inside and outside South Africa; and the Danish Refugee Council wanted to support the Peter Coxan-committee (later 'Ephesus House') working with education for refugee students in Swaziland.

After the meeting the Ministry concluded that Danish support should fall into the following three categories:

1. education inside South Africa,
2. education for refugees, and
3. other sorts of assistance to refugees.[1]

The TS looked into the Nordic equivalents to the Danish 'Apartheid Committee', and arranged a meeting with the Secretary General of the Norwegian Refugee Council and with an official from the Swedish Government Aid agency SIDA.[2] They provided details about Norwegian and Swedish support, and at the meeting the three countries exchanged information and experiences, in particular about Coxan in Swaziland, IRCOZ in Zambia and high schools in Lesotho and Botswana that all three countries were considering supporting. Through Danish staff at a development project in Zambia, research was also done on IRCOZ and on the refugee organization 'International Rescue Committee' in Botswana led by a Commander Cunningham, who was reported to have expressed that 'communists and the likes should be sent back to [South African Prime Minister] Vervoerd who knows how to deal with them'. IRCOZ was judged positively, whereas Cunningham's organization was never discussed again.

TS then suggested that Denmark should support the following:

— IDAF and SACHED on 'education inside South Africa',
— Peter Coxan's committee in Swaziland on 'education for refugees',
— IRCOZ under the umbrella classification 'other sorts of assistance to refugees'.

---

1. Memorandum. 27 January 1966. MFA 6.U.566
2. Minutes form meeting, 2 February 1966 after visit to Copenhagen by Vilhelm Bøe, General Secretary of Norwegian Refugee Council ('Norsk Flyktningeråd') and Chairman of the Norwegian 'Spesialutvalget for Sørafrikansk Flyktningeungdom' (the equivalent to and model for the Danish 'Apartheid Committee') and by Thord Palmlund, SIDA (the Swedish government development assistance agency), Secretary for SIDAs Consultative Committee on Humanitarian Assistance. MFA 6.U.566.

Finally, it was decided to support the WCC for purposes covering all three areas.[1]

This proposal was discussed at the second meeting of the Apartheid Committee on February 11, and was approved by the NGO members. In terms of volume, the Committee agreed to allocate DKK 100,000 to IDAF, 62,000 to WUS, 54,000 to the Coxan Committee and 34,000 to IRCOZ. Support to the WCC was agreed on in principle, but postponed to the 1966/67 budget year as the WCC application was of a very general character, and a more detailed one was expected the following year.[2]

The second Apartheid Committee meeting also discussed the framework for future allocations. The TS sketched the guidelines: The original application from the Minister to the Finance Committee was not to be taken too literally. The intention behind the application had not been to restrict allocations to refugee and/or education purposes, the Ministry explained. Accordingly, the Ministry informed IDAF that it could also apply for funds to support legal aid inside South Africa.

Not surprisingly, the NGOs agreed that there should be as few restrictions as possible. They also agreed on the three support categories put forward by the Ministry, but maintained that South Africans inside South Africa were in the greatest need, and that the number of refugees who had fled the country was limited. The NGOs also wanted to assist the political struggle in Rhodesia and the Portuguese colonies. The Ministry agreed to consider this, and two years later the appropriation was expanded to cover the whole region, starting with scholarships to Rhodesian students. Finally, the NGOs suggested that the allocations were made public, hoping that it would strengthen public awareness and the organizations benefiting from the allocations would be recognised as partners by a Danish ministerial body.[3]

The TS Board was informed about the Apartheid Committee allocations at its next regular meeting a week later, on February 18, 1966. The Board was the body formally in charge of all development assistance, but as the Apartheid Appropriation was a separate allocation on the annual state budget, the TS Board had no formal influence. Formally, the TS now had an independent function as the secretariat for the Apartheid Committee and the Apartheid Appropriation. Some coordination was needed, especially during the first years, when TS funds supplemented the Apartheid Appropriation.

Volume 1965–1971

The Apartheid Appropriation ended the 'anonymity' of Danish aid to Southern Africa, but it was not the only allocation to the region in 1965/66. As shown,

---

1. Note to the Minister. 4 February 1966. MFA 6.U.566.
2. Minutes, meeting 11 February 1966. MFA 6.U.566.
3. Ibid. Announcing allocations in detail would remain restricted, as the Ministry wished to keep domestic criticism of Ministers as low as possible.

DKK 250,000 from TS funds went to the new UN 'Educational programme for South Africans' under the Secretary General. Yet another DKK 250,000 of TS funds also went to IUEF, through a similar procedure to the 1964 grant. The total amount given in 1965/66 totalled DKK 750,000. Over the coming years the Apartheid Appropriation grew slowly but steadily. In 1966/67 the amount was at DKK 300,000, and it then grew annually by DKK 100,000 until 1970/71 when it reached 700,000. Then, in 1971/72, the Appropriation jumped to DKK 1,5 million.[1]

The real increase was in fact bigger than these figures indicate. Some activities first funded by the Apartheid Appropriation were later transferred to TS budget lines as regular bi-lateral or multi-lateral development assistance, up to 1973. This was the case with scholarships and assistance to UN programmes. This procedure continued for some years. From 1974 all Danish allocations to Southern African were integrated into the expanding Apartheid Apropration.[2]

Another interesting multi-lateral budget-line item was support to the refugee 'Mozambique Institute' in exile in Dar-es-Salaam in Tanzania. Sweden had started supporting it in 1966, and invited other Nordic countries to do likewise. In 1968 Denmark allocated DKK 430,000 as multi-lateral support through the UNHCR, and again allocated 500,000 in 1970 and 1971 before the allocation was funded from the Apartheid Appropriation from 1972. As the money was allocated as development assistance, approved by the TS Board, it was not discussed by the Apartheid Committee. Nor is it found to have been discussed politically or in public. It must be concluded that this support to education of exiles in Tanzania, as one of several multi-lateral allocations, did not concern anybody although it went to activities of a liberation movement. As such, this support was not a result of NGO initiatives like the 1971 support to an ambulance to MPLA nor of political initiatives like the large scale support to liberation movements from 1972.[3]

Establishing a track for the future

The double nature of the Apartheid Appropriation, as both humanitarian and political, existed from the beginning. The declared intention to end the 'anonymity' of Danish assistance was clearly political: through the Apartheid Appropriation Denmark openly stated its disapproval of apartheid racism and its repressive consequences. Its creation was a signal to Pretoria, to liberation movements and to the South African public about Danish views. Internationally and in the UN, Denmark, together with the other Nordic countries, pro-

1. Figures from TS/Danida's annual reports and development assistance applications to the Standing Financial Committee. For further details, see tables.
2. For support to the UN funds, WUS and IUEF scholarships, education for refugees in Swaziland and the Mozambique Institute, see tables for UN, WUS, IUEF and for Danish Refugee Council.
3. On support to MPLA and other national liberation movements, and Foreign Minister Hartling later referring to the Institute see Chapter 3.

filed itself as an advocate of human rights, a critic of racism and oppression and a supporter of resolutions and other actions by the UN system.

In other contexts the humanitarian and non-political character was emphasised: the funds allocated through the Apartheid Appropriation went to the education of refugees and other activities that enjoyed universal consensus. Not even the Danish community in South Africa, criticising the Danish initiative of interfering with the internal affairs of another country, nor the white South African public, could openly object to educational programs helping desolate fellow human beings to educate themselves. This aspect was central in the way Denmark responded to these groups.

This contextual shift of emphasis, between political and humanitarian, was repeated when domestic criticism of Danish assistance grew in the 1970's, in particular from the conservative opposition in Danish politics. And when official policy was criticised by the left, for being too weak, the political character and political impact could again be stressed.

Chapter 3

'To' or 'Through'? Denmark Supporting National Liberation Movements

From the beginning, Danish official support to Southern African NGOs enjoyed wide domestic consensus, regarding both its humanitarian substance and its political perspective. In 1971, the support gradually began to include national liberation movements engaged in political and military struggle against the Southern African regimes. At first this was hardly noticed by anyone outside the Apartheid Committee and the Ministry of Foreign Affairs. Only later, from the end of 1971 and onwards, was the political dimension of the humanitarian support highlighted and used politically on the international scene. It then attracted national and international attention and was intensely debated by the domestic opposition.

The Social Democrat K. B. Andersen, Minister of Foreign Affairs from 1971–73 and 1975–78, was a key figure in this development and he more or less came to symbolise the more active Danish approach, intended to put more political pressure on the Southern African regimes.

But K. B. Andersen never actually changed the key procedures or the core 'substance and practice' of the Danish support. It was in fact his predecessor, the liberal Minister of Foreign Affairs (1968–71) Poul Hartling, who started supporting the national liberation movements. Hartling represented the centre-ringt 'VKR-Government' that at this point had been in office for three years.

1971: The first grant to a national liberation movement

On January 28, 1971, the Apartheid Committee was routinely gathered to discuss how the following year's Apartheid Appropriation funds should be allocated. The national liberation movements SWAPO, ZANU and MPLA, from what are now Namibia, Zimbabwe and Angola, were among the applicants.[1]

All the NGO representatives on the committee recommended accepting these applications as 'they [the national liberation movements] carry out important humanitarian activities that well benefit those in need of help'.[2] The NGOs argued that the movements could channel Danish humanitarian assistance to liberated areas and refugees in exile. The three applications were made in rather general terms, seeking funding for medicine, school materials etc. The

---

1. ZANU application 2 February 1970, MPLA application 16 December 1970, SWAPO application of 23 December 1970. MFA 6.U.566.
2. Minutes from meeting of the Apartheid Committee 28 January 1971 (no date). MFA 6.U.566.

Ministry, represented by Danida (formerly the Technical Secretariat for Development Assistance (TS)), did not make any reservations or comments at the meeting. In accordance with usual practice, the largest allocations were granted to existing refugee, legal aid and scholarship programmes, through IUEF, WUS, IDAF and DanChurchAid. But the Apartheid Committee also decided to set aside DKK 50,000 to ZANU and/or SWAPO through IUEF, and 50,000 to MPLA through WUS. The funds were to be released if and when sufficiently detailed applications were received through these NGOs.[1]

After the meeting other parts of the Ministry administration expressed some anxiety as to whether or not this kind of support to national liberation movements would be in accordance with the existing lines of practice. The Political Department in the Ministry commented that 'Support to liberation movements constitutes an innovation'.[2] After considering what was known about the movements in question, the relevant UN resolutions and Per Hækkerup's original description of the purpose of the Apartheid Appropriation, the Political Department concluded that such support would still lie within the four criteria listed for Danish official assistance:

— No military assistance,
— Confirmation by UN that the support would not violate other countries' internal affairs,
— Neighbouring countries accepting transport through their territories and
— OAU acknowledgement of the movements in question.[3]

It was concluded that the existing practice of supporting humanitarian activities through the Apartheid Appropriation would not be jeopardized, as long as the NGOs involved would 'convert' the Ministry funds into medicine, food aid and relevant utensils before it reached the liberation movements so that Danish cash could not be used for military purposes. It was also discussed whether it would be diplomatically well advised to communicate this decision directly to the movements and if they, technically, would be best advised to apply through Danish or international NGOs. The Ministry feared that direct letters to the movements could be interpreted as official Danish recognition, and that the movements would use the exchange to strengthen their international position. However, as the Ministry had already written to ZANU on a previous occa-

---

1. Internal Ministry note 2 March 1971 listing the allocation recommendations made. MFA 6.U.566.
2. Internal notes by the Political Department, 18 February, 5 March and 10 March 1971. MFA 5.Q.293, also filed under 6.U.566. About the three liberation movements it was noted: 'MPLA is one of the three most important freedom movements in Angola and is supported mainly by Eastern countries and so-called progressive African countries... ZANU is one of two rivalling freedom movements in Southern Rhodesia. ZANU, operating mainly from Tanzania, is mainly supported by China. ZANU is recorded to have conducted minor active guerilla activities against the illegitimate Smith regime. SWAPO is one of the freedom movements in Namibia; it represents the largest and most densely populated part of Namibia.'
3. Regarding Hækkerup's appropriation application, see Chapter 2.

sion, it was decided that direct letters from the Ministry would not be inappropriate.[1]

The Ministry's hesitation shows that there was no full political recognition of the national liberation movements at this point in time. It was against official policy to do anything that could be interpreted as an official recognition of the movements. On the other hand, the decision to support them was an indirect recognition of the importance of their humanitarian and educational activities.

Only MPLA responded to the letter from the Danish Ministry. In July 1971, through WUS-Denmark, it delivered a detailed application for an ambulance, a Land Rover, worth DKK 50,000.[2] To release the money would not cause any administrative problems, as the allocation was already prepared through the Apartheid Committee's decision in January and later approved by the Political Department in the Ministry. But, once again, there were second thoughts. The ambulance could quickly be stripped of its medical equipment and used for military purposes that would violate Danish principles of not providing arms or equipment to parties in conflict. The Ministry wrote: 'If Portuguese authorities learned this, they could argue that Danish arms exports policies are not being administrated objectively'.[3] They feared it would damage the Danish long-term position regarding the need for peaceful solutions to colonial conflicts in Africa. Consequently, the Ministry suggested that the money should be used for medicine and medical equipment instead of an ambulance. Minister of Foreign Affairs, Poul Hartling, agreed with the Political Department on this reservation and approved the modification of the MPLA allocation.[4]

WUS-DK was informed about the decision but disapproved. They tried to bypass it by sending a request to Minister of Culture and Development Assistance, Kristen Helveg Petersen. The Apartheid Appropriation was under the Minister of Foreign Affairs and was not Petersen's responsibility, so the move would probably have failed. However, general elections were called in September, before the two Ministers even had the chance to discuss the matter. After the change of government, the Stockholm based MPLA representative to the Nordic countries visited Danida in November to discuss possible support to MPLA, and he asked if the 50,000 could be used for the ambulance as well as for medical equipment. A few hours later, after seeking approval from the new Minister of Foreign Affairs, K. B. Andersen, Danida responded positively.[5]

The Political Department established that the grant was to be considered, that it was humanitarian in substance, and would benefit individual victims of

1. Internal notes by the Political Department, 18 February, 5 March and 10 March 1971. MFA 5.Q.293, also filed under 6.U.566. Note of 22 March 1971. MFA 5.Q.293.
2. Application from WUS/MPLA 27 July 1971. MFA 6.U.566.
3. Internal note Political Department,, 6 August 1971, with Danida (formerly the TS) continuation of 24 September. MFA 6.U.566/8
4. Internal note in Danida (former TS) 28 July 1971.
5. Note 4 November 1971 on visit to the Ministry of Foreign Affairs by Nordic MPLA representative A.A.Neto the same day. MFA 6.U.566.

The first Danish support to a natonal liberation movement, a Land Rover ambulance for MPLA in Angola, on a tour around Denmark to acknowledge the joint donations from the 'Afrika-71'/WUS-campaign and the conservative/liberal government, 1971. (Photo: Ibis)

Portuguese colonialism and warfare. It was not a grant to cover running costs for the MPLA. Technically, the MPLA was considered to be a contractor, a second link together with WUS-DK, channelling the humanitarian aid between the Danish Ministry of Foreign Affairs and the individual refugee.[1]

In other words, the grant was presented as business as usual. In fact, nobody outside the Ministry administration and the members of the Apartheid Committee took any notice, as the formal procedure had not been changed. However, the fact that MPLA itself would run the ambulance, outside the direct control of WUS-DK, actually made this grant more 'direct' than those following K. B. Andersen's political expansion of the appropriation in the years to come.

The MPLA grant can be seen as an indicator of a general political goodwill towards the liberation movements, from across the political spectrum in Denmark. The question is if it represented a genuine change of position—indicating a positive attitude towards supporting the movements as an administrative arrangement, but negative about getting too much public attention about it. If so, the explanation may be that for the Danida members of the Apartheid

---

1. Exiles or internally displaced persons in Angola.

Committee, the humanitarian substance of the MPLA allocation was so obvious that they did not consider it a radical change of procedure.

According to internal documents from the Political Department the MPLA allocation, '[was] not presented to the Minister, in accordance with previous practice'.[1] The Committee's decisions were labelled 'recommendations' ('indstillinger') and could thus be considered advice to the Minister.[2] This indicates that the Apartheid Appropriation was politically relatively uncontroversial until March 1972. It represented quite a modest amount of money, and its humanitarian purposes were backed by a broad political consensus. It is not uncommon for Ministry officials to be in charge of issues that are not considered politically hot, even if they are formally the Minister's responsibility.

With the MPLA support, this changed. The Political Department was made aware of the grant on February 18, 1971, and three weeks later Danida gave a written summary of the Apartheid Committee's meeting on January 28. On March 5, the Political Department concluded that the political implications of the support 'seem to go beyond previous government policy. Laying the matter before the Minister seems necessary at this stage...'[3]

On one copy of the TS summary it is underlined in pencil that the MPLA and ZANU/SWAPO allocations will be given *'through WUS'*, *'through IUEF'* and as *'humanitarian work'*. The note is also marked 'to be put before the Minister'.

On March 10 the Political Department summarised its hesitation in a note, stating '..the critical point is that support remains only 1) for humanitarian purposes and 2) through international organizations.' On March 19 the word 'agree' is added, with Minister Hartling's signature.[4]

Denmark and its Nordic counterparts

Denmark was not the only country considering assistance to the Southern African liberation movements in the beginning of the 1970s. Sweden had already started supporting PAIGC in Guinea Bissau and was planning on expanding. Norway was debating a similar move. When the Nordic Ministers of Foreign Affairs met for their bi-annual meeting in Stockholm, April 1971, the Danish Minister of Foreign Affairs Poul Hartling expressed his concerns about whether or not supporting national liberation movements in their struggles

---

1. Internal note 18 February 1971. MFA 6.U.566.
2. As shown in Chapter 2, the procedure until 1971 was that the Apartheid Committee proposed the annual allocations to the TS/Danida board. Then Ministry officials handled the administrative details concerning the grants, before the Minister signed the final application to the Financial Committee. Hækkerup's original application for the appropriation stated that 'administration [of the allocation]... should be left to a committee of representatives...' and even if there is no direct conflict between this wording and the actual procedure, it is still rather remarkable considering its official status as 'advisory to the Minister', as showed for instance in minutes from the meeting 28 January 1971. MFA 6.U.566.
3. Note 2 March 1971. MFA 6.U.566.
4. Note 10 March 1971. MFA 5.Q.293.

against recognized governments was in conflict with international law. At the same time he expressed the importance of providing humanitarian aid to liberated areas where government channels would be of no help. This dilemma reflected the struggle going on in his Ministry, trying to decide if, and how they should support MPLA, ZANU and SWAPO.

Andreas Cappelen, the newly appointed Norwegian Minister of Foreign Affairs, announced that Norway planned to support liberation movements and wanted to strengthen its criticism of Portugal's colonial policy, partly within NATO. Norway looked favourably at applications for health and educational assistance to liberation movements in the Portuguese colonies. It is not clear if Cappelen actually meant that the Norwegian assistance would be going directly "to' the movements', but what Cappelen said was that such assistance would follow previous patterns of allocation procedures. Until 1973, this meant Norwegian support would continue to be channelled through UN, IDAF, Norwegian and international NGOs.[1]

In Norway, a 'Special Committee for Refugees from Southern Africa' had been established in 1963 to administrate official funds for humanitarian purposes to victims of apartheid. As shown in Chapter 2, this committee served as a model for the Danish Apartheid Committee. But whereas the Danish committee gradually developed to handle more forms of support from the Apartheid Appropriation, the Norwegian one remained strictly humanitarian, supporting mainly schools for exiled South Africans and IUEF scholarship programs. The UN 'Education and Training programme for Southern Africa' and 'Trust Fund' channelled the money, and some limited assistance to IDAF was funded directly from the Norwegian Ministry of Foreign Affairs. The Norwegian Refugee Council served as the secretariat for the 'Special Committee' until 1972 when it was taken over by the Ministry of Foreign Affairs (and not by the official development agency NORAD). NORAD, however, had decided in 1970 that refugee groups and activities run by 'organizations and movements working for national and social liberation' should not be excluded from receiving regular development assistance. This included liberation movements in liberated areas. A government 'white paper' from the end of 1971 confirmed this, with references to the many UN resolutions in the field, but due to a change of government in 1972 it was not decided by parliament until February 1973.[2]

---

1. 'Uddrag af 'Resumé av förhandlingarna vid det nordiska utriksministermötet i Stockholm den 26–27 april 1971". MFA 6.U.566. Memo: Nordisk samrådsmøte 26. mai 1971 and attached table of Norwegian assistance, 1969–1971. At the coordination meeting Norwegian officials said that the applications they had received from liberation movements were for educational and heath activities similar to the Mozambique Institute in Tanzania, but within liberated areas in Guinea Bissau and Mozambique. Mixing support to the Institute established in exile and activities in liberated areas inside the Portuguese colonies did not help Danish decisions. MFA 6.U.566.
2. On the Norwegian debate, see Eriksen (ed.), 2000, pp. 49–56 and attached table of Norwegian assistance, 1969–1971.

At the same meeting Sweden's Minister of Foreign Affairs, Torsten Nilsson, explained that there was wide political backing in Sweden for support to national liberation movements. Sweden had already transferred its first direct official humanitarian aid to the liberation movement in Guinea Bissau in the annual budget 1969/70, and Nilsson said that the Swedish support was increasing and was soon going to include MPLA in Angola.[1]

Nilsson had been in favour of funding national liberation movements for a long time. In April 1967 the Social Democratic party branch ('Arbetarekommun') in Stockholm, chaired by Nilsson himself, had adopted a resolution and a statement—the latter formulated by Nilsson—that 'requested the government to increase economic support to the liberation movements of the Portuguese colonies'. This was in an addition to the existing support to Frelimo's Mozambique Institute in Tanzania.[2]

On December 10, 1968, Nilsson gave a speech at a seminar, stating that the Swedish state would support liberation movements. As a party member Nilsson had personally been involved in formulating the request, but the reply was given in his position as Minister. The speech was published in a press release and widely discussed in Sweden in the following days, and it was immediately reported to Denmark by the Danish embassy in Stockholm.[3]

In February 1969, during a debate in the Danish parliament, the Left Socialist Party ('Venstresocialisterne') asked Minister of Foreign Affairs Hartling to start supporting national liberation movements struggling against Portuguese repression. They also referred to Nilsson's December speech. Hartling replied that 'Denmark worked and supported within the UN framework and according to the UN Charter... and had supported the Mozambique Institute through the UNHCR'.[4]

A few weeks after the new Danish Social Democratic government took office in October 1971, the Prime Minister, the Minister for Trade and the Minister of Foreign Affairs, K. B. Andersen, travelled to Norway and Sweden, mainly to discuss and coordinate the attitude on the European Economic Community (EC) that Denmark was in the process of joining. During the meetings with the governments in Oslo and Stockholm there was also time for Andersen to discuss support to Southern Africa with his colleagues.

1. 'Uddrag af 'Resumé av förhandlinggarna vid det nordiska utriksministermötet i Stockholm den 26–27 april 1971'. MFA 6.U.566. Memo: Nordisk samrådsmøte 26 mai 1971.
2. The Stockholm initiative was referred to by Bengt Ahlsén, member of the party branch and Chairman of the Stockholm South Africa Committee, in an undated letter to Niels Munk-Plum, Chairman of the Danish Anti-Apartheid Committee who, as a member of the Apartheid Committee forwarded a copy to the Ministry in letter of 1 May 1967. MFA 6.U.566.
3. Letter of 10 December 1968 from the Danish Embassy in Stockholm to the Ministry of Foreign Affairs with copy of press release with Nilsson's speech. For more on the Swedish debate, see Sellström 1999a, p. 234ff.
4. Folketingets Forhandlinger 19 February 1969. About the first—and rather unnoticed—support to Frelimo 'Mozambique Institute', see Chapter 2, p. 37.

In Norway, Deputy Minister of Foreign Affairs, Thorvald Stoltenberg, informed Andersen that the Norwegian government had moved a proposal to grant NOK 700,000 for printing equipment, medical equipment etc. to national liberation movements, in addition to the existing humanitarian grant. He also explained that the Norwegian government had reluctantly agreed to Telli Diallo and the OAU-delegation's wish that an OAU conference on liberation in Southern Africa could be held in Oslo. It had been emphasized to the delegation that Norway did not want to be involved as organizer or host, but might contribute financially together with the other Nordic countries. Andersen said that the Danish Social Democratic party had been informed by Diallo that representatives of the Social Democratic parties in other countries would be among the organizers. He did not like the idea, and the two governments agreed that the Nordic UN associations should be involved along with the World Council of Churches and other NGOs, rather than the governments.[1]

In Stockholm, the new Swedish Minister of Foreign Affairs, Krister Wickman, informed Andersen about Swedish assistance to PAIGC in Guinea Bissau and MPLA in Angola. At the most, Swedish assistance to national liberation movements in Africa had totalled SEK four million. Sweden contributed between SEK one and two million for medical and educational equipment to the PAIGC, and Portuguese reactions to the support had been few. Sweden had suffered no cancellations of business orders or other economic consequences. Wickman further explained that supporting the PAIGC and MPLA had never given any administrative problems. Also, in terms of international law, it was official Swedish policy that there was not much difference between support given directly to a liberation movement or through international organizations.

The UN organizations supported the national liberation movements, and Sweden's position was that 'as long as the UN General Assembly can support the movements, so can Sweden'. Regarding the proposed OAU conference, Sweden was generally very positive about the idea, but did not intend to 'provide sponsorship'. It would rather give a minor financial contribution.[2]

These meetings provided Andersen with information that allowed him to continue to push for an increase in Danish support to national liberation movements. Sweden already did support them, and Denmark's NATO partner Norway seemed to be following suit. Administratively, Sweden had no bad experiences with the movements, and politically Sweden's way of referring to UN General Assembly Resolutions—that could otherwise have been disputed because they were not unanimous and only partly confirmed by the Security Council—was a particularly useful reference for Denmark.

---

1. Minutes from meeting 25 October 1971 between Norwegian Minister of Trade Per Kleppe, Deputy Minister of Foreign Affairs Thorvald Stoltenberg and Danish Minister of Foreign Affairs K. B Andersen. MFA 6.U.566.
2. Minutes from meeting 26 October 1971 between Swedish Minister of Foreign Affairs Krister Wickmann and Danish Minister of Foreign Affairs K. B. Andersen. MFA 6.U.566.

K. B. Andersen later referred to the Norwegian and Swedish support in parliamentary debates, but in his 1983 memoirs he does not. He does not mention any Nordic inspiration for the Danish Social Democratic party programme of 1969 either. At this point, in 1983, the cold war of course dominated the political debate while support to national liberation movements had ceased to be a core political issue.[1]

Danish NGO initiatives: 'Afrika-71'

By 1971, the NGO and grassroots initiatives on South and Southern Africa from the first half of the 1960s had lost pace. The apartheid regime seemed to have managed to clamp down effectively on internal protests. News from South Africa no longer made headlines in Europe like it used to. Events in Rhodesia were not considered significant enough to interest more than a few. Its 'Unilateral Declaration of Independence' from Britain in 1965 and the subsequent UN sanctions in 1968 had drawn some attention, but the issue focused on international law and did not have much public appeal. The 'new left' had its eyes on national liberation and anti-imperialism in Vietnam, rather than on Africa.

The Danish organizations concerned with Southern Africa continued to be the ones established in the first half of the 1960s: the Anti-Apartheid Committee, the Danish Youth Council (DUF) and the umbrella structures South Africa Fund and the Council for Southern Africa (Fællesrådet). The consumer boycott campaigns in 1960 and 1963 had successfully mobilized the Danish public, but a later major fund raising and information initiative only managed to draw about the same amount that had been invested in the campaign.[2]

The money was distributed through IDAF (the South Africa Fund was the Danish branch of IDAF) and the individual committee members then paid the deficit out of their own pockets. This experience did not inspire other fund raising initiatives. However, the magazine 'Sydafrika Kontakt', started by the Anti-Apartheid Committee, continued to be published, and was taken over by the Council for Southern Africa from 1967.[3]

At its General Assembly in 1968, held in Uppsala, Sweden, and its Central Committee meeting in Canterbury, England the following year, the World Council of Churches (WCC) established the 'programme to Combat Racism'. Later, in 1972, a Danish branch was established, called the 'Kirkernes Raceprogram'. The initiative came late, considering the events in South Africa in the 1960s, but in Denmark it served as a continuance between the media focus on the big trials against ANC and other leaders in the mid-1960s, and the renewed media interest after the Soweto uprising in 1976.[4]

---

1. See Chapter 5.
2. See Chapter 2 about popular attention on Southern Africa in the 1960s.
3. Interview with Ole Bang 12 May 1997.
4. Talk with Leif Vestergaard, April 1997, see also Chapter 4.

The left's anti-imperialist stand on Vietnam, however, indirectly helped in opening Danish eyes to the anti-colonial struggles in Southern Africa. The anti-American protests of Danish youth and students were partly incited by the feeling that Denmark wrongly sided with American imperialism through its membership in the military alliance NATO. Critics held that the alliance also legitimated fascist regimes in the NATO countries Greece and Portugal, and Portuguese colonialism.

The Danish Students' Council (DSF) played a central role in the new left, and as the student constituency of DSF was radicalised by the student protests, the DSF leadership also changed. The new leaders saw the struggle against imperialism and exploitation in the third world as part of the radical struggle within Denmark, against NATO membership, the arms race and even against what was considered the capitalist content of university textbooks. Danish progressive students experienced African guerrilla fighters as their brothers in arms, and this provided a basis for mutual solidarity. Support to African liberation struggles was perceived as more that just 'aid'. A defeat of imperialism in Africa would also weaken the same forces in Denmark.[1]

One of the DSF activities was the World University Service-Denmark (WUS-DK), a branch of WUS-International until 1970. Through DSF, WUS-DK became one of the NGOs represented on the Ministry of Foreign Affairs' Apartheid Committee from the start in 1966, actively advocating an increase of the annual allocations from the Apartheid Appropriation. WUS-DK was funded both from the Apartheid Appropriation and through Danida. These funds were channelled mainly through WUS-International for SACHED and other scholarship programs in South Africa and Rhodesia.[2]

The radicalisation of the Danish students' movement, as well as the year 1971 being declared International Year for Action against Racism by the UN, made WUS-DK decide that they wanted to create a framework for more active political solidarity work. At the WUS-International assembly in 1970 in Ibadan, Nigeria, WUS-DK proposed that the organization should start supporting the liberation movements in its next four-year programme. The proposal was not adopted because such a decision would endanger the ongoing scholarship programmes in South Africa and Rhodesia. Consequently, the Danish delegates reorganized WUS-DK as an independent organization on their return to Denmark. No longer a branch of the international organization, they considered themselves affiliated with WUS-International. In this position WUS-DK would be free to support liberation movements without damaging WUS-International's programs, which WUS-DK could still continue to raise money for.[3] Together with the high school students' organizations (Danske Gym-

---

1. Interview with Peder Sidelmann, 3 December 1996, and talk with Klaus Wulff, 17 September 1996.
2. DKK 242,000 from the Apartheid Appropriation 1966–69 plus Danida funding scholarships for refugees in exile.
3. Interview with Peder Sidelmann, 3 December 1996.

nasieelevers Sammenslutning, DGS) and Internationalt Forum (IF—the youth wing of the Danish UN-association (FN-Forbundet)) the 'new' WUS-DK started preparing a one-year information and fund raising campaign about racism, colonialism and neo-colonialism in Southern and Eastern Africa, called the 'Afrika-71' campaign. 'Afrika-71' approached national liberation movements in Southern Africa for contacts and information material. Since most of the other Danish organizations supported activities in South Africa and Rhodesia, 'Afrika-71' decided to focus on the Portuguese colonies. Denmark's partnership relations with Portugal through NATO and EFTA made this a rational choice, both morally and as a point of departure for the domestic information campaign. Of the liberation movements in the three Portuguese colonies, Frelimo in Mozambique already had a well-established relationship with Sweden and received Swedish support, and PAIGC in Guinea Bissau was outside of the Southern Africa sphere. The Angolan movements FNLA and MPLA were contacted, and MPLA was 'found to be the least regionally focused', the one with the best national backing—and 'as the decisive factor the one that gave the best response'.[1]

MPLA also had specific programs and plans for their humanitarian and educational work and could identify needs for health equipment including a mobile clinic/ambulance, agricultural implements, 'bush school' facilities in liberated areas and the upgrading of its '4 de Feveiro' secondary school in exile in Congo Brazzaville. The MPLA Secretary of Organization and Training, Lúcio Lara, was also willing to come to Denmark from Brazzaville and boost the campaign.[2]

In the 'Afrika-71' campaign, WUS was in charge of the research on and contacts with the liberation movements. 'IF' was in charge of the information policy. Of the three organizations behind the campaign, 'IF' was the only one with individual membership. Several of their members were both enthusiastic and had in-depth knowledge of Africa and issues like racism and colonialism. The high school students (DGS) worked on the fund raising, including an arrangement at the end of November called 'Operation Day's Work', where high school students all over the country contributed the equivalent of one day's wages to a humanitarian purpose.[3] This was the second time 'Operation Day's Work' was arranged in Denmark, and the former government had already decided upon 'Afrika-71' as one of the receivers.[4]

Most Afrika-71 campaign activities took place from September to November 1971. The campaigners arranged seminars and had specialized lecturers touring the country, including high schools. The tour started with Börje Matt-

1. Ibid. *Politiken*, 17 October 1971. 'Afrika-71 Evalueringsrapport' by Otto H. Larsen. Internal evaluation sent to Ministry of Foreign Affairs, May 1972. MFA 5.Q.293.
2. Interview with Lúcio Lara in Sellström 1999b, pp. 18–21.
3. The first Danish 'Operation Day's Work' was arranged in 1969, raising money for a Unesco School Project in Zambia.
4. *Politiken*, 15 September 1971. *Kristeligt Dagblad*, 22 October 1971.

son from Finland, speaking at the University of Copenhagen about his experiences from areas in Angola liberated by MPLA, about their civil activities and about the Portuguese use of chemical weapons. A week later Abdul Minty, Political Secretary in British Anti-Apartheid Movement, gave a lecture about South African imperialism in the region and explained how arms supplies from Western Europe would help South Africa to undermine possible NATO measures to prevent Portugal from using NATO equipment in Africa. In October, the ANC scholar Ruth First toured Denmark for five days and gave lectures about the situation in South Africa and how apartheid interacted with Portuguese colonialism in a situation resembling Vietnam.[1]

The campaign produced a newsletter on the anti-colonialist struggles and initiatives of national liberation movements in the region and of the independent governments in the front-line states. The paper included contributions from the Danish political parties. They all denounced apartheid and spoke favourably about Danish humanitarian assistance in general, but only the socialist parties emphasized the political role of the liberation movements and promoted Danish contacts and support.

Afrika-71 also published a book with economic and political background information about the situation and history of Southern and Eastern Africa. The book tried to answer two questions: 'What is it like in Southern Africa?' and 'Why is it like that?'. Part of the answer to the last question was that 'Denmark is engaged in a military partnership with Portugal in NATO and an economic one in EFTA. The ruling class in Portugal benefits greatly from Portuguese affiliation with these organizations as arms supplies from or via NATO countries help continue the war in Africa—and Portugal enjoys preferential arrangements in EFTA'.[2]

The book further expressed hope that

> knowledge of the conditions may contribute to understanding Denmark's role as a minor pawn in the overall game that allows brutal oppression and exploitation of the people in certain countries whereas those in other countries are overwhelmingly confident with society structures that are considered natural, but are based on exploitation of peoples in for instance Southern Africa.

Finally, posters and giro-forms were printed and distributed for information and fund raising:

> ... It is no longer sufficient to rely on pressure on Danish authorities to make them radically re-consider Danish involvement in Southern Africa. We shall have to make extra-parliamentary steps—to support liberation movements out of our own pockets... Every day we hesitate to contribute will make it more difficult for those who struggle to remove

---

1. *Politiken*, 15 and 24 September and 7 and 13 October 1971.
2. Bislev et al. 1971, Foreword (no page numbering) and p. 69.

fascism with arms and afterwards to eradicate poverty and ignorance... Schools must be built..., devastating diseases must be fought... and food must be produced through agricultural production in liberated areas.[1]

Twenty local study, information and fund raising groups were established across Denmark along with similar groups in many of the high schools. They discussed the Afrika-71 book, organized for one of the five Afrika-71 poster exhibitions that toured the country to be displayed at the local library, facilitated the touring lecturers, collected money and handed out information material in the street. As an example, even the small town Haslev, south of Copenhagen, was visited by Ruth First and the Swedish journalist Knut Andreassen, who had travelled in areas in Guinea Bissau liberated by PAIGC. The theatre group 'Rimfaxe' made a play about the conditions in the Portuguese colonies, performed at schools and in the streets. And at the end of the campaign the MPLA Land Rover ambulance, funded mainly from the Apartheid Appropriation, toured Denmark with the drama group and a poster exhibition.[2]

In October an OAU delegation, headed by Secretary General Telli Diallo, visited the Nordic countries. They stopped in Denmark to mobilize political backing and financial support for the OAU's increased efforts against Portuguese colonialism, initiated at a meeting in Lagos in December 1970. The delegation met twice with the Afrika-71 campaign and a possible private Danish committee for support to the OAU was discussed. The delegation had more difficulties arranging meetings with Danish government representatives, as Denmark was in the process of installing a new government after the September general elections. However, the new Prime Minister Krag and Minister of Foreign Affairs K. B. Andersen, together with the Director of the Ministry, received the delegation as one of their first official assignments. Telli emphasized the importance of the role the Nordic countries played in the UN and that the OAU countries intended to coordinate resolutions etc. with the Nordic group. He proposed that Denmark should support the OAU's own funds for support to national liberation movements, as well as the public committee for support. Andersen promised to consider this, but it never materialized. The main reason was that the liberation movements in question later expressed that they preferred direct assistance. They were also concerned about the lack of resources of the OAU administration for handling such funding.[3]

1. 'Afrika-71' campaign 'newspaper', giro material, posters etc. Internal WUS memo by Knud-Erik Rosenkranz 4 September 1979 summing up previous WUS campaign experiences, Ibis 26.1 and 28.1. 'Afrika-71 Evalueringsrapport' MFA 5.Q.293. Afrika-71 posters were designed and produced by the socialist collective of artists 'Røde Mor'.

2. *Næstved Tidende,* 6 September 1971. *Kristeligt Dagblad,* 22 October 1971. For Knut Andreassen's trip to Guinea Bissau with MP Birgitta Dahl, see: Sellström 1999a, p. 431.

3. Report 2 January 1971 from the Danish embassy in Lagos to the Ministry, referring to the OAU meeting and resolutions in Lagos 9 to 12 December 1970. MFA 5.Q.293. *Politiken,* 10 and 11 October 1971. Minutes, 12 October 1971: Meeting between OAU delegation (General Secretary Telli and Algerian ambassador Shadal) and the Director of the Ministry of Foreign Affairs. MFA 5.Q.293.

On October 28, the 'Afrika-71' campaign arranged a conference with representatives from each of the political parties in parliament at the University of Copenhagen. The campaign tried to get the Minister of Foreign Affairs to participate, but he declined. The representative of the Social Democratic Party declared that Denmark should criticize Portugal more firmly, and that the party was preparing direct support to humanitarian and educational activities of the liberation movements. 'Swedish and Norwegian experience showed [that] such support was possible', he said. The amount of Danish support was not settled yet, and 'a decision about whether or not some of the funds should be channelled through OAU would be a matter of OAU administrative efficiency in this respect'.[1] As agreed with Afrika-71, Lúcio Lara visited Denmark in November. He participated in seminars and press meetings. He also met with Danida, and discussed the idea of building a new secondary school for exiled students in Congo Brazzaville. Danida responded that official Danish assistance to the project was possible, but would require an application with more details about the project and its administrative procedures. Lara's visit was not high profiled. While in Copenhagen he stayed with WUS activist and Afrika-71 Campaign Secretary Peder Sidelmann on the university campus and used public transport to get around.[2]

The campaign managed to raise a total of DKK 446,000. DKK 343,000 came from the high school students' Operation Day's Work in October. The rest was contributions by some 1500 individuals, and the combined result was considered quite substantial.[3] It reflects a re-vitalized focus on Southern Africa in the general public, linked to the left's mobilization on Vietnam and the perceived need for international solidarity against the mechanisms of imperialism and neo-imperialism at play. Unlike in the 1960s, the issue at stake was not primarily violations of human rights by South Africa's apartheid regime, but the situation in the Portuguese colonies. In this sense Afrika-71 was a campaign 'closer to home' than the campaign in the 60s, as one of the main motivating factors was the role and responsibility of Denmark's political and economic alliance with Portugal. The Afrika-71 campaign also coincided with a change of attitude in the Social Democratic Party, a development that had been going on since 1969. When the party took office in October 1971, the campaign was encouraged to go ahead. WUS, IF and DGS had the moral and political convic-

---

1. Internal ministerial notes describing the Afrika-71 seminar 28/10. 28 October 1971, MFA 5.Q.293 and 2 November 1971, MFA. 6.U.566.
2. Ministerial note 30 November 1971, minutes from visit to the Ministry by Lúcio Lara and Klaus Wulff. MFA 6.U.566. Interview with Sidelmann, 3 December 1996. On the Congo school project, see below.
3. *Kristeligt Dagblad*, 22 October 1971. Information letter August 1973 to Afrika-71 campaign contributors. WUS 10.1.

tion that something needed to be done, and this developed into concrete action in an environment of political possibilities and financial prospects.[1]

The Social Democrats and the national liberation movements

At its 30th party congress in June 1969 the Social Democratic Party had adopted a so-called 'Action programme' to profile itself on domestic and international issues while in opposition. The programme pledged the party's support to national liberation movements and to their struggle for political, economic and social independence in a number of countries, South Africa, Rhodesia, Mozambique, Angola, Guinea Bissau and Vietnam.[2]

The issue was given high priority. In a section called 'Denmark and international relations' the support for liberation movements followed the paragraph on the United Nations and preceded issues like general development assistance and continued NATO membership. K. B. Andersen later explained in his memoirs that the focus on national liberation movements was a recognition of 'world history [..] no longer being confined to Europe', after World War II.[3] The Nazi Germany occupation of Denmark during World War II was not a distant experience, and the Danish resistance movement played an important role in the Social Democratic Party's way of understanding and morally siding with the movements in Africa.

Domestic political currents were also an important context for the 1969 Social Democratic congress. The end of the 1960s and the 1970s was marked by political left wing mobilization, especially among students and youth. USA was strongly criticized for its involvement in Vietnam and its role as 'the world policeman'. Inspired by the Vietnam War, 'Solidarity with oppressed peoples of the Third World' had become a political slogan. Students' manifestations often included attacks on imperialism in South East Asia, Latin America and Africa. The NATO military alliance was considered a tool for imperialism, and the Danish membership was questioned. Denmark had joined the alliance in 1949, for a period of twenty years. In 1968, students occupied the University of Copenhagen and the same year a fraction of the People's Socialist Party (Socialistisk Folkeparti) seceded and formed a new party, the Left Socialist Party (Venstresocialisterne). This had eventually led to the fall of the SF-supported Social Democratic government the same year. The Social Democratic Party had come under pressure from the new left and was forced to strengthen its positions including issues like international relations and solidarity. Last, but not least

---

1. Letter 24 October 1971 from 'Afrika-71' to Minister of Foreign Affairs K. B.Andersen referring to a meeting between Wulff and Sidelmann with Andersen in June 1971, four months before the change of government. MFA 5.Q.293.
2. Det nye Samfund: 70ernes Politik ('A New Society: Policy of the 1970s'). The section: 'Danmark tilhører Verden ('Denmark belongs in the World').
3. Andersen, 1983, pp. 14–16.

the party was in opposition and subsequently in a much freer position to formulate a radical policy than it would have been in government.[1]

During 1969 and 1970 the Left Socialist Party repeatedly proposed that the Danish parliament should officially recognize the African national liberation movements and financially support them, but without backing from other parties.[2]

During the budget debate in the winter 1970 – 1971, discussing the budget of 1971/1972, the Social Democratic Party proposed an increase of the Apartheid Appropriation by DKK 5 million, 3.5 million more than the 1.5 million suggested by the government. At the third and final budget reading, on March 30, the proposal was raised again, but not passed.[3]

On September 21, 1971, general elections were called. A new Social Democratic government was formed, under Jens Otto Krag. The Prime Minister presented the government's programme in parliament on October 19, and in his inaugural speech he announced that the government intended to 'expand the humanitarian and educational support to oppressed peoples and groups through international organizations and liberation movements'.[4]

During the following parliamentary debate there were no comments on this particular issue from the conservative and liberal parities in the outgoing government. The immediate reaction came from other quarters. The NGO campaign 'Afrika-71' was just starting, and welcomed the pledge to support liberation movements, but, as could be expected, considered it too modest: 'The Social Democratic Party has previously proposed that 5 million be allocated to liberation movements, but that will not suffice.' 'With our Afrika-71 campaign we will focus on how unbalanced this is out of a development assistance budget of between 600 and 700 million. Liberation movements have since 1961 proved to be the only and the most efficient organizations to change conditions in the developing countries... In less than ten years Frelimo in

---

1. *Politisk Revy* no 118, 21 February 1969 and no 130, 29 August 1969. The magazine 'Politisk Revy' became a forum for the new left. Upon the killing of Frelimo President Eduardo Mondlane it ran articles in 1969 on Portuguese colonialism emphasising the importance of NATO equipment, along with an interview from *The Guardian* with Amilcar Cabral from the Guinean liberation movement PAIGC, listing aircraft models supplied by NATO member countries and used in Portugal's colonial struggle. An issue later in 1969 had an interview with MPLA representative Humberto Traca under the heading 'NATO struggling against us'.
2. Question to the Minister of Foreign Affairs 19 February. Foreign Policy debates 29 May 1969 and 19 February 1970. Folketingets Forhandlinger 1968–69, 4165 and 7154. Folketingets Forhandlinger 1969–70, 3707.
3. During the opening of the budget debate 10 December 1970 the Social Democratic Party proposed that the parliament should 'recognise the right of liberation movements in Africa, Asia and Latin America to fight for independence and also for economic and social justice.' Folketingets Forhandlinger 1970/71, F 2267. Together with the People's Socialist Party (SF) the Social Democrats moved an amendment (no. 68) to allocate 5 million extra 'for humanitarian relief work in the form of support to liberation movements'. This was repeated during the final budget reading on 30 March 1971. Folketingets Forhandlinger 1970/71, F 5231.
4. Folketingets Forhandlinger 1971–72. F 34.

Mozambique have built more schools in liberated areas than the Portuguese colonial regime did in centuries'.[1]

Liberation movements with human faces: 'But, we knew them'

K. B. Andersen describes and explains Denmark's support to national liberation movements in his memoirs as follows: 'Now, why all this interest for Africa? Because... the white man has made so many mistakes in Africa that it has been important for me to try to understand the liberation struggle, not in an East–West perspective but on the basis of its own background and premises'.[2]

The main point for Andersen is that liberation movements in Southern Africa were nationalist, not communist. Their cause, he explains, was not to create a communist society as a replica of the Soviet Union or China, but to get rid of colonialist oppression or state racism. He sees this as a just cause, in line with Danish general support to de-colonization and with the Danish struggle against the German occupation during World War II. Finally, he was certain that the movements would, eventually, succeed. On these grounds Denmark was morally obliged to support the struggle:

> As Minister, I was often criticized for promoting support to liberation movements... [as they were said to be] non-democratic, communist infiltrated movements. The point that I repeatedly made was that we would not be doing Western democracy any favours by turning our backs on the liberation movements. On the contrary: it would send them directly into the arms of communism.[3]

To Andersen, supporting the national liberation movements was not supporting a global communist movement that the West—and certainly the Social Democratic movements in the West—was against. On the contrary: if the West failed to meet its obligations, the movements would have no other option but to look for help in communist countries, and with conditions or propaganda attached, the movements might be influenced or forced or cheated into forming communist societies. K. B. Andersen pointed to Egypt as an example of how a developing country could become part of the Soviet sphere of influence. The West had denied Egypt the agreed financial assistance to build the Aswan Dam, which made Egypt turn to Moscow for help. In Andersen's opinion it was not only morally wrong but simply also politically unwise of the West not to assist the movements. It is with some satisfaction that Andersen quotes US Secretary

1. MFA 6.U.566. *Kristeligt Dagblad*, 22 October 1971. Interview with Peder Sidelmann, 3 December 1996.
2. Andersen 1983, p. 49–59. A politician's memoirs must be expected partly to serve as retrospective conclusions to justify political decisions. However, Andersen's writings stand the test when details and general analyses are compared to primary sources, and they bring forward arguments for why the Social Democratic party took on this policy.
3. Ibid, pp. 14–50. Political commentator Carl Otto Brix in a biographical essay on Andersen as Minister of Foreign Affairs describes the two focus areas in his time in office to be: the relations to Africa and developing counties, and adjusting Denmark's foreign policies to the EC before and after joining in 1972. Brix, 1994.

MPLA President Agostinho Neto with Social Democratic Party Secretary and later Minister of Foreign Affairs K. B. Andersen in a Copenhagen restaurant in 1970. (Photo: Hans Strømsvik/Polfoto)

of State Henry Kissinger for expressing his regrets to Andersen about not having given Africa priority, nor having been able to understand the situation as a complex fight against colonialism and racism rather than a cold-war situation.[1]

Personal contact with leaders of the liberation movement was crucial in reassuring Andersen and the Social Democrats that the movements were nationalist and not communist. MPLA President Agostinho Neto has a prominent place in K. B. Andersen's memoirs. Andersen was elected Party Secretary in January 1970, and in that capacity he hosted Neto's visit to the Danish Social Democratic Party the same year. Neto toured the Nordic Social Democratic Parties, mainly on the initiative of the Swedish party and the Social Democratic Youth in Sweden.[2] Andersen was clearly impressed:

> Neto made a strong and remarkable impression... through his dignified appearance and well-considered opinions. He was also known for his often-gentle poetry about the liberation struggle and about its victims... I also remember Neto's wise answers at a press conference during his visit. Against the background of the harsh press debate during Neto's visit, about the horrifying and aggressive people of whom he was said to be the leader, it

1. Andersen 1983, p.20.
2. For Neto's visit to Sweden and first official Swedish contacts with MPLA, see Sellström 1999a, p. 424–429.

is interesting to study the nature of the requests he made: medicine, sheets, powder milk, agricultural implements and clothing for children, women and old people.[1]

Most of the Social Democratic Party shared the impression of the liberation movements as pre-dominantly nationalist, not communist.[2] Their main aim was seen as humanitarian. They wanted social and economic development, which, however, was not possible before national liberation was achieved. Contact with the movement leaders was also facilitated by the increase of UN resolutions from 1960 and onwards that made such meetings possible according to international law. The reference to the Danish resistance movement 1940–1945 helped the struggle for independence to be seen as legitimate. 'We knew them', as Kjeld Olesen, former party official and Minister of Foreign Affairs puts it. Olesen organized Oliver Tambo's visit to Denmark in 1960 and 1962.[3]

Steen Christensen is another example. The Secretary of the Social Democratic 'Workers' Solidarity Fund' (established at the 1969 Social Democratic party congress) had studied in Britain in 1967, together with exile members of ZANU, including future post-independence Ministers. His impression is that: [The liberation movements' communist rhetoric] 'could be applied as it would suit specific international situations. It was possible to get support from the Soviet Union or from China if you said the right things and that is what they did. But—as far as I know them—they would never dream of setting up 'people's communes' in Zimbabwe or in South Africa'. 'Knowing these people over many years, it is obvious that they wanted their national independence.'[4]

---

1. Andersen 1983, p. 17. Poems by Neto were published in Denmark in Per Wästberg's anthology 'Afrika Fortæller' in 1962, translated from the Swedish version from 1961. When the prominent periodical 'Den Ny Verden', specialising in global social, economic and cultural issues started in 1964, it published Neto's poems in its first issues. Den Ny Verden. 1.1, 1.2 (1964), 2.1 (1965).
2. Ibid. K. B. Andersen also refers to leaders of African states in his memoirs. Nyerere is quoted for expressing that the perception is wrong that African liberation movements are communist, and for quoting the 'Lusaka Manifesto' that 'the peoples of Mozambique, Angola and Portuguese Guinea are not interested in communism or capitalism, but in their freedom'. The Lusaka Manifesto (printed in Legum and Drysdale, 70: p. C41ff) though adopted in April 1969 is not referred to by Andersen as background for the Action Programmeme of the Social Democratic Party from June 1969.
3. 'We had talks till late in the night during his visits, including about the resistance movement in Denmark. The ANC was not controlled form Moscow. Communists were very active in the ANC, but they were so in the Danish resistance movement during World War II... Together with K. B. Andersen I talked to Neto, he was no communist but a great humanitarian... The liberation movements used a lot of rhetoric but behind that we knew better... They could not mobilise on 'democracy' in places where there had never been democracy, they had to formulate an ideological basis about oppression and social injustice and how you get rid of that... Many built on an ideology inspired by marxism, but so did the Danish Social Democratic Party in its early days.' Interview with Olesen 21 August 1997.
4. Interview with Steen Christensen 9 January 1997. Christensen became the Social Democratic International Secretary 1980–1984, and Party General Secretary 1984–1997.

Minister of Foreign Affairs, K.B. Andersen announces his expansion of the Danish humanitarian support to national liberation movements in Southern Africa, November 1971. (Photo: Scanpix/Willy Lund)

'Millions to African freedom struggle'

The drafting of the new government's annual budget for 1972/73 started while K. B. Andersen was still visiting Norway and Sweden and while 'Afrika-71' was busy with its campaign activities. The new government wanted to allocate DKK 6.5 million (about USD 1 million) to the Apartheid Appropriation and have its budget line name changed to include the national liberation movements. On his return, Andersen discussed the expansion of the Appropriation with the administrative heads of the Ministry. They saw no formal problems in supporting the movements using normal Danida procedures, as long as the appropriation did not go to 'un-specified' support, such as administration.[1]

In mid-November, after Andersen had participated in the annual UN General Assembly, he called a press conference upon his return and announced the expansion of DKK 5 million to be allocated 'to African liberation movements'. The newspapers reported it under headings such as 'Million Kroner Support to African Freedom Struggle'.[2] Interestingly, it did not raise any political or public debate at this stage. In a letter to the members of the Apartheid Committee the

---

1. Internal note 2 November 1971 with section of draft budget. Internal note 8 November 1971 on discussion 3 November between the Minister, the Director of the Ministry and the Heads of Departments for Danida and for the Political Department about Apartheid Appropriation procedures. MFA 6.U.566.
2. *Berlingske Tidende*, 18 November 1971. *Aktuelt*, 18 November 1971.

Ministry wrote that the new government's initiative would mean 'a new Apartheid Appropriation'.[1]

The way these changes were presented, and the fact that they had been included in the government's inventory of new policies, shows that Andersen and the new government considered them a substantial political innovation, or at least wished to present them as an innovation. On the other hand, the response Andersen got from his senior officials at their meeting on his return shows that the administration did not. Given the allocations already agreed upon to make a grant to the MPLA (and ZANU and SWAPO) at the beginning of the year and the considerations that followed, this is not a surprise.[2] At the meeting, Andersen agreed that the substance and practice of the Apartheid Appropriation would stay largely unchanged.

The Apartheid Appropriation was now four times as large as in the previous budget. The question of whether the plan for such an expansion was 'just' quantitative or if it was qualitatively an innovation—'a different appropriation' with a different, wider purpose— is central to the nature of Denmark's official support to Southern Africa. The expansion can be measured in two ways: on its actual 'substance and practice' that did not change much, or on its political impact that did develop. If seen as a continuation of the existing support, the assistance was still humanitarian, an indication that Denmark still pursued the policy started in 1964. If seen as an innovation, it meant that Denmark had embarked on a new and more high-profil policy.

Already during its preparations, the administration in the Ministry of Foreign Affairs envisaged confusion about this two-sided nature. To clarify matters, the Ministry administration produced an internal memorandum outlining the background and defining the future practice for the allocation. This document was later used as a reference for what could be supported and what could not. Previous support from the Apartheid Appropriation was described, including the 1971 grants to MPLA and ZANU/SWAPO and the international law implications were discussed. Non-interference was stated as a basic principle for Danish foreign policy, but it was considered 'justifiable to maintain' that this principle would not be violated by humanitarian assistance to Southern Africa, as 'UN Security Council resolutions invite member countries to provide support or at the least specify that oppression ought to cease'. The Minister's formulations were analysed, and the document concluded that 'the new appropriation' would technically be a continuation of previous support. It could, however, be considered a step beyond existing practice in terms of working relationships, as the support could now be channelled through liberation move-

---

1. Letter 29 November 1971 from the Ministry to members of the Apartheid Committee. MFA 6.U.566.
2. See p. 43

ments in addition to international organizations, as long as 'direct contributions in cash to the movements' was avoided.[1]

What should be noted is that according to the memo, the 'humanitarian and
educational' support could now be 'channelled *through* organizations and
national liberation movements', but not *to* either category.[2] The organizations
were seen as vehicles for support to individual beneficiaries. After this overall
assertion, the memorandum states that the full title of the Apartheid Appropriation, including the new amendment '...and to liberation movements', implies
three possible procedures for allocations:

> a) to international organizations for support of their own activities;
> b) via international organizations to humanitarian and educational activities of national
>   liberation movements and
> c) directly to national liberation movements, to their humanitarian and educational
>   activities.

This shows that the practical administrative procedures actually did allow for
support 'to' and not through the receiver. But the conclusion does not:
'Whereas the first two options do not require any special control, the latter
does as regards Danish authority control with the correct utilisation of the
funds'. This would mean that 'direct contributions to liberation movements
would not be an option'. In other words, the latter of the three options was in
reality not considered relevant, despite the fact that the changed title for the
allocation referred to international organizations and liberation movements as
equal options for assistance. With these definitions the Ministry administration
established that the 'substance and practice' of official Danish assistance would
not be changed.

The memorandum was communicated to K. B. Andersen who did not make
further comments, although its conclusions narrowed what was expressed in
the 1969 Social Democracy working paper, in the government's opening speech
in October and at his own press conference in November. However, Andersen
would soon make good use of the memo's narrower definitions.

The memorandum came to define the future Danish support to Southern
Africa. It specified that allocations would take place according to the existing
procedures and criteria. However, in the public as well as the political debate
there was a strong understanding that national liberation movements would
from now on receive funding. This confusion is apparent in the most inconsis-
tent use of the prepositions 'to', 'through', 'via' or 'direct' in the debates that
followed. No distinctions were made to clarify if the liberation movements
were beneficiaries, channels for support or partners, whereas the Ministry

---

1. Memorandum, 10 December 1971: 'Humanitær og uddannelsesmæssig støtte gennem befrielses-
   bevægelser' ('Humanitarian and Educational support through national liberation movements')
   MFA 6.U.566. The Security Council Resolutions referred to were 277 (1970) on Rhodesia, 269
   (1969) on Namibia, 282 (1970) on South Africa and 290 (1970) on the Portuguese colonies.
2. Ibid. The italicizing here of prepositions and in the following text is done in this study for the
   purpose of analysing the character of Danish support.

memorandum had established that practice would continue to be the latter. The debates would focus on whether or not Denmark should support, or was supporting, the liberation movements directly.[1]

Reactions to Andersen's expansion

Andersen expanded the volume of the Apartheid Appropriation, but did not change its form or nature. His loud announcement of the expansion created quite some political turbulence domestically, but it also helped Denmark draw international attention to the situation in Southern Africa and the role played by the liberation movements. The double nature of the appropriation was important to Andersen, because it provided political space on the international scene, and at the same time protected him from domestic criticism, by underlining the humanitarian and educational purposes of the appropriation.

From March 6 to 20, 1972, just before the third reading of the budget in parliament, K. B. Andersen visited Tanzania, Kenya and Zambia to discuss Danish development assistance and other relations between Denmark and these countries, as well as the situation in Southern Africa in general. At a press conference he seized the opportunity to announce the expanded Apartheid Appropriation, which he presented as new and as support 'to' the liberation movements. In Tanzania, he also visited the Mozambique Institute and met with Frelimo and the OAU Liberation Committee. In Zambia he met with the MPLA.[2]

In the Tanzanian–Danish communiqué, released as a press statement, K. B. Andersen said that 'the Danish government and people support the legitimate attempts of peoples in Southern Africa to liberate themselves, and intend to continue herewith'.[3] The Tanzanian press complimented Andersen for having shown more interest in Africa's biggest problem than any previous visitor on the same political level. In Zambia, Andersen emphasized in speeches and interviews that Denmark believed in self-determination of the South African peoples.[4]

---

1. Budget proposal 30 November 1971, Folketingets Forhandlinger 1970/71, D1.
2. Minutes from meetings 8-9 March 1972 between K. B. Andersen and OAU Assistant Executive Secretary Ahmed Sidky, between K. B. Andersen and Janet Mondlane and between Andersen and Samora Machel. Minutes from meeting 13 March 1972 between Andersen and Agostinho Neto. MFA 5.Q.293.
3. Press release (Danish version) 10 March 1972. Reuters news agency telegram 10 March 1972 quoting Tanzanian newspaper *The Nationalist* the same day. MFA 5.Q.293.
4. Manuscript for speech: Response to Zambia's Minister of Foreign Affairs E. Mudnenda at reception 13 March 1972. KBAaba. Cable 14 March 1972 from Danish embassy in Lusaka referring to Andersen's speech. MFA 5.Q.293. President Kaunda welcomed the Danish policy as it was a Western country and said it could strengthen those in the liberation movements that sought to avoid Eastern dominance. 'MPLA and Frelimo are genuinely independent movements that have worked to remain free of Eastern influence. This is part of the reason why OAU have backed up these two movements. Minutes 14 March 1972 from meeting the same day between President Kenneth Kaunda and Minister of Foreign Affairs Andersen. MFA 5.Q.293.

Director of the FRELIMO Mondlane Institute in Dar-es-Salaam, Janet Mondlane, meets with Minister of Foreign Affairs, K.B. Andersen, in Copenhagen, 29 March 1972. Andersen had visited the Institute a few weeks earlier during his trip to East African countries where he announced Danish support to national liberation movements. Denmark supported the Institute from 1968 following an invitation from Sweden. (Photo: Polfoto)

Portuguese newspapers—largely controlled by the government—strongly condemned K. B. Andersen's statements, his visits to Frelimo and the Mozambique Institute in Dar-es-Salaam. Andersen was an issue in the Portuguese press for several weeks, and the Danish embassy in Lisbon received several threatening letters. Portuguese criticism was further fuelled when Janet Mondlane, the Director of Frelimo's Institute, visited Andersen in Copenhagen immediately after he returned home and on March 28 asked for arms assistance from the West in an interview on Danish TV.[1]

In South Africa the opposition newspaper 'The Star' quoted K. B. Andersen's statements under big headlines: 'Terror Groups offered R12 mill'. The paper had got the figures wrong, as this was the equivalent of the total Danish development aid. South African opposition spokesman Japie Basson criticized Denmark, and the Chairman of the ruling Nationalist Party's Foreign Affairs Group, Paul van der Merwe called the grant 'abhorrent'. A newspaper editorial headed 'Utterly Foolish Action' called the support 'naive' and 'blood money', as it would prevent peaceful solutions. Another editorial in 'The Star' with the heading 'Something Rotten', denounced the grant but also emphasised that the harsh apartheid measures would have to be softened in order to prevent more countries from giving up hope of peaceful solutions. In 'The Cape Times' Prime Minister John Vorster and head of opposition, Sir de Villiers Graaff, both denounced 'the Danes' guerrilla grant', and 'The Argus' ruled out that support would be humanitarian: 'Money given to terrorists is money for murder'.

---

1. Cable 13 March 1972 from Danish embassy in Lisbon quoting newspaper editorials in *Diario de Noticias* 11 March 1972 and *Epoca* 12 March 1972. MFA 5.Q.293. Report 5 April 1972 from the embassy describing official, diplomatic and public reactions in Portugal. MFA 6.U.566.

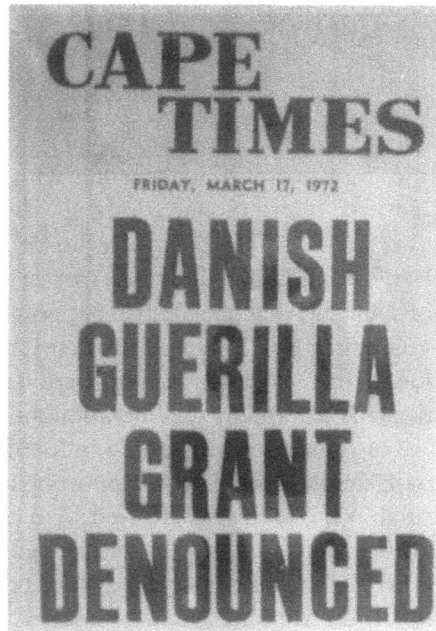

South African newspaper advertisement denouncing Danish support to national liberation movements. March 1972.

South African individuals sent some of these clippings to the Danish Consulate representatives with comments like: 'You should be ashamed of your country.'[1]

The news travelled the world. Nigerian newspapers quoted the Tanzanian press. The Danish ambassador in Cairo reported from a visit to Ethiopia that OAU Secretary General Telli Diallo acknowledged Denmark's support and that the Portuguese reactions were on the front page of the Ethiopian press. The Swedish daily 'Sydsvenska Dagbladet' quoted the strong Portuguese and South African reactions and explained the Portuguese rage as being because Denmark and Portugal were members of the same military and trade alliances, NATO and EFTA.[2]

On March 17, while Andersen was still in Africa, the Portuguese ambassador visited the Danish Ministry of Foreign Affairs claiming that the liberation movements were communists and bandits, and that he had been called home for consultations. The Ministry Director answered by evoking the 'substance and practice' of the support and explained to the ambassador that the Apartheid Appropriation was meant for humanitarian and educational purposes and that cash allocations were not granted, from fear that they might be misused

---

1. Report 20 March 1972 from Danish embassy in Johannesburg and consulate in Cape Town, with news clippings from 16 and 17 March. MFA 5.Q.293.
2. Report 11 March 1972 form the Danish embassy in Lagos. Clipping from Swedish newspaper *Sydsvenska Dagbladet* 18 March 1972. Report 29 March from Danish embassy in Cairo on visit to Addis Abeba. MFA 5.Q.293.

for arms purchases. The ambassador did go home, but he soon returned, and later made no further official protests.[1]

In Denmark the first news comments on Andersen's announcements in Africa were quite positive. The conservative daily newspaper 'Berlingske Tidende' praised the Danish 'humanitarian and educational support to resistance movements' that, together with the general development assistance, gave Denmark international goodwill. The term 'resistance' rather that 'liberation movements' was a positive echo of the Danish resistance movement during World War II. The daily newspaper 'Politiken' criticized the Portuguese press for ignoring that the Danish support was meant for educational and humanitarian purposes. This was the first time the domestic press paid any real attention to the Apartheid Appropriation since the Prime Minister had announced his plans to support the liberation movements in October 1971.[2]

On March 19 an editorial in 'Berlingske Tidende' found however that Denmark should refrain from supporting liberation movements. On the 27th an editorial in the tabloid 'B.T.' told K. B. Andersen 'to keep his nose out of Africa' and asked how it could be guaranteed that the support was not spent on arms.[3]

In the budget debate in parliament on March 23 and in a letter to the editor in B.T. on March 29, K. B. Andersen explained the 'substance and practice' of the expanded Apartheid Appropriation in detail, trying to rectify the impression his statements in Africa had made of Denmark giving support *to* the liberation movements. This was not enough to end the political and public debate, partly due to Andersen. Even when he explained the 'substance and practice' of the Apartheid Appropriation expansion, he kept referring to its political nature, as he had done since his first press conference in November 1971. It was the high profile political side of the Apartheid Appropriation that had such strong effects internationally, and that also fuelled the domestic debate. Andersen tried to explain that the 'substance and practice' would remain largely unchanged, and emphasized how this was in continuation of earlier policy. MPLA, SWAPO, ZANU and the Frelimo Mozambique Institute had already received support under the former Liberal ('Venstre') government.

In April 1972 the debate re-erupted with the news that Danish exports to Portugal and South Africa had been affected. Two industrial orders had been cancelled. The Confederation of Danish Industry wrote to the Prime Minister and demanded that the government covered the losses. Individual private companies wrote to the Ministry of Foreign Affairs and criticized the Danish policy, and the Danish Chamber of Commerce demanded that Danish support must be changed. The Chairman of the Danish Metal Workers Union, the Social Democrat Hans Rasmussen, requested the Social Democratic government to give up its policy as it could jeopardize employment in Denmark. The government

1. Note, Minutes 17 March 1972 from meeting the same day between Portugal's ambassador to Denmark and Director of the Danish Ministry of Foreign Affairs. MFA 6.U.566.
2. *Berlingske Tidende* and *Politiken*, 12 March 1972.
3. *B.T.* 29 March 1972.

rejected the protests, and in the end it appeared that the two export orders in question had been lost before K. B. Andersen's trip to Africa, and had nothing to do with Denmark's policy.[1]

Still, the public was divided. Some newspapers believed that the expansion of the Apartheid Appropriation meant that Denmark would now give support *to* national liberation movements. They saw the movements in a cold war context, as communists and terrorists, and criticized K. B. Andersen for pursuing a costly policy with no other effects than to ruin Danish exports. Others based their opinion on the fact that the 'substance and practice' remained unchanged, and agreed with K. B. Andersen's three arguments: that civilians (in exile, in liberated areas or in prison because of political activities) should not be denied humanitarian or educational assistance because they were in contact with or members of liberation movements; that the cold war arguments did not apply to the African movements; and that any possible negative effects on Danish trade were insignificant compared to the moral obligations of the matter.

Interestingly, Poul Hartling, the Chairman of the Liberal Party (Venstre) and K. B. Andersen's predecessor, criticized the government in public as well as in parliament for 'directly supporting national liberation movements' and for allocating funds that could not be controlled. Under the former government 'money to liberation movements was solely channelled through international organizations', he explained, unaffected by Andersen's explanation in parliament three weeks earlier that the 'substance and practice' would remain unchanged.[2] Hartling—like many others—was confused by Andersen's choice of preposition in 'support to liberation movements' and it indicates a shift internally in Venstre from the policy it had pursued in government to a more critical attitude while in opposition.

Parliamentary debates: 'To' or 'through'?

The annual 1972–1973 budget was passed on March 23,1972, including the increase of the Apartheid Appropriation from DKK 1.5 to 6.5 million. In addition, its budget line title was changed to include the liberation movements. During the debate in the Standing Parliamentary Financial Committee, the liberal and conservative opposition parties moved an amendment where the previ-

---

1. *Information*, 4 and 12 April. *Jyllandsposten*, 12 April. *Politiken*, 12, 14 and 16 April. *Børsen*, 13 and 17 April. *Berlingske Tidende*, 28 April. Letter from Rasmussen to Prime Minister Krag 4 April 1972, answer from Andersen to Rasmussen 8 April. Rasmussen had been approached by Knud Tholstrup, owner of a major company fearing to lose the order for gas facilities for Portugal. In his reply, Andersen offered to meet with Tholstrup to discuss the issue. Letter 22 June 1972 from Knud Tholstrup thanking Andersen for telephone conversation inviting him to a meeting which he declines. KBAaba, Box 21. Letter 13 April 1972 from the Danish Chamber of Commerce to the Minister of Foreign Affairs. Letters 19 April 1972 from Prime Minister Krag to Director of the Confederation of Danish Industry Arnth-Jensen and from K. B. Andersen to the President of the Chamber of Commerce Dan Bjørner. MFA 5.Q.293.
2. *Børsen*, 13 April 1972.

ous year's volume and formulation were maintained, but a majority of the three other parties rejected this.[1] The budget line now said that support could be given 'through liberation movements' and in the presentation of the adjusted budget proposal at the start of third reading, the Social Democratic spokesman said that 'in accordance with the policy of the Social Democratic party the government is proposing to make funds available for humanitarian as well as educational assistance to oppressed peoples and groups, [and] that the assistance can be channelled through international organizations as well as through liberation movements'.[2]

The debate never got beyond the confusion about the two words 'through' and 'to'. The written text said '*through* liberation movements', but K. B. Andersen continued to refer to it by saying '*to* liberation movements'. A spokesman of the liberal opposition party 'Venstre' argued that their amendment to maintain existing practice was the result of 'not wanting to give [funding] *to* liberation movements—it will be difficult to choose between competing movements, it will hardly be possible to control the use of donated funds and it would be a violation of the principle not to give government funding without the consent of the government of the receiving territory'.[3]

Andersen reminded parliament that the opposition's suggested amendment would prevent 'the government proposal to give support *directly through* liberation movements'. He underlined that it was not an innovation 'to give such support *through* liberation movements', and reminded parliament that ZANU, SWAPO and MPLA had already received support 'to humanitarian activities', although '*via* private international organizations'. 'Now such funds can also be channelled *via* liberation movements', Andersen continued.[4]

The confusion continued in parliament a month later in a two-day general debate about Denmark's foreign policy. In his presentation, K. B. Andersen said that Denmark was going to increase the humanitarian and educational support to oppressed peoples and groups 'through international organizations or *directly through* liberation movements.' He underlined that the governments of Kenya, Tanzania and Zambia had all emphasised 'the political and psychological significance it would have if a Western country—and even a NATO member—would make such a step'.[5]

The Conservative spokesman quoted the former Director of the Ministry of Foreign Affairs, saying that 'conflict in a foreign country would always have to

1. Budget proposal and amendment no 74 by 'Venstre' and 'Konservative', Folketingstidende 1971/72 D1. Parliamentary proceedings, third and final reading on 23 March, Folketingstidende 1971/72, F 4067–4173. Interestingly, in August 1971, before the change of government, then Minister of Foreign Affairs Poul Hartling had found DKK 2 million to be an appropriate volume for the appropriation for the coming 1971–1972 budget. Internal note 22 March 1972, MFA 6.U.566.
2. Third reading, 23 March 1972. Folketingstidende F 4068.
3. Parliament proceedings 23 March 1972. Folketingets Forhandlinger F 4099.
4. Ibid. and F 4160–61.
5. Parliament proceedings 19 April 1972. Folketingets Forhandlinger F 4953–54.

be fought between the parties without any interference from other governments... For this reason the Conservative Party was against changing existing
principles for assistance so that it would now come to include humanitarian
assistance *to* liberation movements'. Venstre's spokesman, former Minister of
Foreign Affairs Poul Hartling said that it had previously been Denmark's policy
to support refugees. What the present government was introducing was support even *to* the liberation movements within their home territories. Hartling
referred to Andersen's formulations at the press conference back in November
and during his trip to Africa. Hartling refused to accept the actual budget text
as superior to Andersen's previous oral statements, a compromise that might
have mitigated most of the conservative and liberal criticism. Venstre also
found that distributing official funds behind the backs of 'the actual governments' was a violation of the principle of non-interference, which could not be
accepted, 'regardless of the fact that Venstre dissociated itself from the
regimes'.[1]

Andersen replied that UN Security Council Resolutions denouncing the racist and colonial regimes as illegitimate, provided a platform for Denmark to
extend its support *to* liberation movements, without violating principles of
non-interference. The support would not be unique. African countries were
providing similar support and so were Norway and Sweden, and with larger
amounts than the Danish allocation. Andersen also asked Hartling 'what official backing he had when he allocated funds *to* MPLA, SWAPO and ZANU *via*
IUEF and WUS as Minister of Foreign Affairs'. But on this point even Andersen
was mistaken. Hartling's previous allocations had never been *to* national liberation movements.[2]

Hartling then pointed at the inherent confusion in Andersen's argument.
'On one hand the Minister claims that the government is merely doing what
previous governments were doing, on the other the argument is 'we are doing
something new'.' If 'the new' appropriation really was an innovation, Hartling
was against it. If it was not, he saw no reason to criticize the government, 'but
then again, there would be no basis for the political profiling that has been
done on the issue, neither in Africa nor domestically', he said. 'If the Minister
can't see this difference he really is an old horse as there is a clear distinction in
argument.'[3]

This was a precise analysis and could have clarified things. But the fact that
in the discussion Hartling ignored the fact that liberation movements were
involved when he had allocated funds prevented the confusion from being
solved.

1. Conservative spokesman Østergaard in parliament proceedings 20 April 1972. Folketingets
   Forhandlinger F 5048. Ambassador Nils Svenningsen in *Berlingske Tidende*, 13 April 1972. Parliament proceedings 20 April 1972. Folketingets Forhandlinger F 5062-64.
2. Parliament proceedings 20 April 1972. Folketingets Forhandlinger F 5105–07 and F 5113–15.
3. Ibid. F 5128–29.

Andersen did refer to what we may call the 'to or through' debates in his 1983 memoirs. And even more than ten years later, Andersen mixing things up maintains the confusion. He writes that the expansion of the Apartheid Appropriation 'included allocations also *to* national liberation movements' and that this had taken place even under Hartling, although he subsequently maintains: 'These were very modest allocations and it had not, as we suggested, been directly *to* the liberation movements but *via* international organizations—not government to government [or movements].'[1]

But in 'substance and practice', money was never distributed *to* the national liberation movements. Funds were never given directly to them and they were never the primary project partners for the Ministry. Neither had this been the case under Hartling. What Hartling had started, and what Andersen consolidated was that support *to* NGOs with refugees *as the beneficiaries* could now sometimes take place *in collaboration with* the movements.

Dolisie: NGOs favoured over Unesco

WUS-Denmark's and the 'Afrika-71' campaign had successfully introduced the Portuguese colonies and their national liberation movements—especially the MPLA—into the Danish debate. It coincided and interacted with K. B. Andersen and the Social Democratic Party's move to begin supporting national liberation and the timing proved to be good for both.

Since the end of the 1960s, the MPLA had worked to establish educational facilities similar to Frelimo's Mozambique Institute in Tanzania. For 2–3 years, MPLA had unsuccessfully tried to get funds from Unesco or OAU. MPLA wanted to develop their '4 de Fevereiro' school started in exile in Congo Brazzaville in 1965, and they had already been assigned a building site by the Congolese government near the town of Dolisie. WUS-Denmark was told about the plans soon after it had made contact with MPLA by mid 1971, and the plans were made part of the information strategy of the Afrika-71 campaign.

WUS presented the plans to K. B. Andersen and the Ministry of Foreign Affairs, and discussed them further with Lúcio Lara when he visited Denmark in November to participate in 'Afrika-71'. The Ministry's response came a week later at a meeting with Lara and Klaus Wulff from WUS. The plans and budgets for the project were found to be too sketchy, but the Ministry said it would welcome an application for the 1973/74 budget. After the meeting, WUS suggested to Lara that it could help MPLA produce a detailed application and work as MPLA's partner. Lara went to Sweden and met with the Swedish official aid agency SIDA and a preliminary agreement was made. SIDA would

---

1. Andersen 1983, p. 23–24.

Visit to the MPLA refugee school in Dolisie, Congo, by MPLA President Agostinho Neto and Secretary of Organisation and Planning Lúcio Lara in 1973. WUS Representative Peder Sidelmann (later UNICEF manager of the school) and Construction Manager Karl Johan Holt (to the right) show the visitors the site. (Photo: Peder Sidelmann)

fund the school's running costs after its completion, through Unesco as the project partner.[1]

During the Afrika-71 campaign WUS had recruited architects, civil engineers, draughtsmen and other technicians who supported the campaign and wanted to do solidarity work. They established themselves as a voluntary planning group within WUS and in March 1972, WUS leader Peder Sidelmann and one of the architects visited Congo where they had meetings with the Congolese government and the MPLA. They measured the building site, researched available building materials and prices, had meetings with the Congolese authorities etc. and collected necessary information for a professional project proposal.

This coincided with Andersen's trip to Africa and his meeting with Agostinho Neto in Lusaka; they did not discuss the Dolisie project as such, but Andersen mentioned Danish uncertainties about supporting liberation movements and wished to know Neto's opinion about possible channels of funds. Neto was delighted about Danish support to MPLA and mentioned the need

---

1. Ministry notes 22, 24 and 30 November about the MPLA project and Lara's visit to the Ministry 30 November. MFA 6.U.566/8. WUS Newsletter 1 August 1972 describing the 'Angola Institute' and its background. WUS 16.1. 'Afrika-71 Evalueringsrapport'. Internal evaluation of the campaign, no date, sent to Danida start of 1972. MFA 5.Q.293.

for medical assistance in the liberated areas in Angola, but he did not comment on the possible channels for the assistance.[1]

Soon after his trip to Congo, Sidelmann met with Danida and reported that the findings in Congo had proved to be good for the project and that planning was going ahead. He also said that SIDA had been approached for support but had not responded, but he did not mention that he had met a fact-finding mission from Unesco also investigating the building of the MPLA school at Dolisie. Danida said that it was generally positive about the project, that it would soon call a meeting of the Apartheid Committee to discuss it and the possible allocation of funds from the Apartheid Appropriation and that it would contact SIDA to coordinate the support from the two donors.[2]

WUS had their hopes up, but on April 26, 1972, WUS was told at a meeting in Danida, with the participation of SIDA and Unesco, that it had been decided that Unesco should build the school. SIDA Director Stig Abelin explained that they preferred to cooperate with Unesco rather than with WUS and did not expect MPLA to have any preferences. SIDA was hesitant to give a lot of money to a young and inexperienced organization and also wished to involve Unesco in working with the national liberation movements. WUS objected that its estimated price was 75 per cent of Unesco's, that its project preparations had come far in comparison to Unesco's and that the MPLA wanted construction to start as soon as possible. Danida had not made up its mind, but said it trusted WUS to be able to handle the project.[3]

The coming weeks were busy, both for WUS and for Danida. Danida recognised that SIDA had administrative preferences for Unesco, because the money could then be allocated from existing budget lines whereas the WUS option would mean finding extra money. SIDA rated WUS-Denmark as 'private persons', and they did not have any procedure for donations of this kind. Danida also understood the point that involving Unesco would mean a politically important breakthrough in the involvement of UN bodies working with national liberation movements.

It was SIDA that had financed the Unesco mission to Dolisie that WUS met in Congo. MPLA had sought funding for the school for some years and there had now been a breakthrough in two quarters. Altogether, Danida was positive about Unesco building the school, as it would be administratively safer, also in

---

1. Minutes 14 March 1972 from meeting in Lusaka 13 March between K. B. Andersen, Agostinho Neto and Zambian Minister of Foreign Affairs Mudenda.

2. Interview with Afrika-71 Secretary Peder Sidelmann, 3 December 1996. Letter 7 April from WUS to the Ministry summing up the Dolisie project process and asking for a meeting. Minutes of meeting 19 April 1972 between WUS and Danida. MFA 6.U.566/8. The Apartheid Committee had met on 14 March and allocated about DKK 1.5 million of the coming 1972/73 budget, equal to the previos year's budget, but had postponed allocated the new extra 5 million. Minutes, no date. MFA 6.U.566.

3. Interview with Sidelmann, 3 December 1996. Minutes from meeting 26 April at Danida with SIDA, Unesco and (the last half of the meeting) WUS. MFA 6.U.566/8. There is no correspondence between Danida and SIDA in the material for the one week period between WUS' visit to Danida on 19 April and the meeting on 26 April.

the light of some recent critical comments from the audit department about lack of detailed planning of some construction projects. However, *if* schedules were kept to, WUS would be cheaper and faster than Unesco, but so far no detailed plans had been presented. This uncertainty made K. B. Andersen approve the Unesco option in early May, provided that WUS would still have some part to play in the project, for instance as supplier of teaching materials to the school. Later, SIDA informed Danida that it was prepared to cover all expenses, both the construction and the running costs, through Unesco, to get the project going.[1]

WUS recognized SIDA's argument about its lack of experience and suggested to Danida on May 7 that a project board be established with veteran NGOs in the Apartheid Committee, who had agreed to monitor WUS' management of the project. The next day, after weeks of working late hours by the working group of architects, WUS submitted final project plans and an application for DKK 3.24 million for construction of the Dolisie project, with a full budget of DKK 4.85 million. Further, the volunteer architects asked their employers to write a statement confirming that the quality of the project was in no way inferior to a commercial project. This was followed up by a meeting in Danida with representatives from the employing companies. Finally the involved architects in the working group made it clear that they for professional reasons and reasons of principle could not accept their work being handed over to and likely changed by Unesco.[2]

Political action followed. MPLA wanted a quick start of the construction work, whether it was to be WUS or Unesco that would manage the project, and had informed Danida about this in April. After its disappointments at the April 26 meeting with Danida, SIDA and Unesco, WUS needed stronger MPLA references and contacted Lúcio Lara to arrange that Agostinho Neto send a telex, in which he specifically emphasized that MPLA wanted WUS to carry out the project. MPLA also asked SIDA to inform Danida that MPLA preferred WUS, as it seemed to be faster than Unesco. In mid-May the Apartheid Committee met again and discussed the Dolisie project. Danida presented an estimate saying that choosing Unesco would be safer, would guarantee the participation and contributions of SIDA and would involve Unesco in working with the liberation movements. But the NGO members of the committee backed the WUS option and recommended it to the Minister with the arguments that WUS would be cheaper, that Unesco would probably waste the plans already made, that much of the public backing behind the project—as had manifested itself in

---

1. Internal notes 4 and 10 May 1972. MFA 6.U.566 and internal notes 8 and 17 May and 14 June 1972, MFA 6.U.566/8.
2. Letter from WUS to Danida 7 May 1972. WUS 16.4. Application from WUS to Danida 8 May 1972 MFA 5.Q.293. Letters from Krohn and Hartvig Rasmussen to WUS 10 May and to Danida 1 June 1972 confirming the quality of the planning project. WUS 16.4 and MFA 6.U.566/8. Note 14 June 1972, MFA 6.U.566 and 17 May, MFA 6.U.566/8. The project board came to include representatives from Danida, WUS, the WUS planning group and one of the architect employers.

the 'Afrika-71' campaign and fund raising—would be lost, that it seemed certain that SIDA would still fund running costs after the completion, and that WUS and the Danish Refugee Council threatened to reconsider their financial inputs to the project as it would lose its public appeal if the support 'went to Unesco rather than directly to MPLA through WUS.'[1]

Armed with these arguments Klaus Wulff and Peder Sidelmann from WUS visited K. B. Andersen in early June, in their opinion the only person who would be able to change the decision about giving the money to Unesco. They argued that WUS would be morally obliged to go back and inform its contributors, the Afrika-71 campaign participants, the press and the public that the collected funds could not go to the project in the form in which it had been presented during the campaign. The Danish government seemed to trust a UN organization more and was not interested in contributions from volunteers and popular NGOs. A week later WUS was summoned to a new meeting with Danida and was informed that WUS would build the school after all.[2]

Dolisie became WUS-Denmark's first development project and laid the foundation for its future as one of the major development Danish NGOs. SIDA and Danida's concerns about WUS not being able to handle the complex construction project were proven wrong. After a slow start, where containers shipped to Dolisie were emptied of equipment and filled with sand by Portuguese authorities during a stop that the ship made in Lisbon, there were no serious problems in the construction process. On the other hand, it was not fast either, and building the school took three years instead of the planned two. However, it was cheaper than expected. DKK 250,000 remained when construction was finished, and with Danida and the Apartheid Committee's approval, the money was used for building an extra block for housing more students. Even then there was money left to return to Danida.[3]

After the school was completed Unesco ran it with SIDA funding and—at the request of MPLA—with Sidelmann as its administrator. In 1973, WUS-Denmark became engaged in another major pre-independence project with MPLA. WUS was asked to assist with the transport of humanitarian aid still

---

1. Letter from MPLA Committee Director Lúcio Lara 5 April 1972 to Danida. MFA 5.Q.293. Letter from WUS to Danida 7 May 1972. WUS 16.4. Interview with Peder Sidelmann 3 December 1996. Minutes, no date, from meeting of the Apartheid Committee 18 May 1972. MFA 6.U.566.

2. Neither the Neto telex nor material on the meeting between WUS and Andersen was found in files available for this study; information from interview with Sidelmann, 1996.

3. Letter 26 July from the Danish ambassador to Congo (based in Zaire) reporting from his visit to the Dolisie school. His impression about planning, the quality of construction, the enthusiasm and working relations between WUS, MPLA and the Congolese authorities was positive—'it is my clear impression that work is seriously and enthusiastically carried out'. WUS 16.4. Auditors examined the Dolisie books in 1974 and had no comments. Audit reports 31 August and 2 September 1974. WUS 16.4. Application 11 November from WUS to Danida for using surplus for extra construction, WUS 16.4; approved by the Apartheid Committee in 1974 included in appropriation application (Finansudvalgets Aktstykker) no 58 of 1974/75. Letter 16 March 1977 from WUS to Danida with closing financial reporting. WUS 16.4.

stored in the port of Dar-es-Salaam, which could not be distributed to refugee camps in Zambia at the border with Angola. The aim of the project was to deliver vehicles and mechanical equipment and provide education for drivers and mechanics for the driving and maintenance of the vehicles. WUS applied for funds from the Apartheid Appropriation, but with the advice of K. B. Andersen the focus was predominantly humanitarian, focusing on supplying clothes, blankets, medicine etc. to the refugee camps. The vehicles and training were a component linked to it for transportation—and could afterwards serve to move the stored goods waiting at Dar-es-Salaam. The project began in 1974 and continued after the Independence of Angola in 1975.[1]

WUS-Denmark had good contacts with the MPLA from the start, and the MPLA and Lúcio Lara's readiness to take the inexperienced students from WUS-Denmark seriously, were crucial for the fund raising for the exile school in Congo, both as a boost to the enthusiasm and documentation during the 'Afrika-71' campaign and for convincing the Minister and the Danida administration in the Ministry of Foreign Affairs. By setting good administrative standards it paved the way for other projects supporting national liberation movements through NGOs. When domestic criticism later arose, it was possible for K. B. Andersen and the Ministry of Foreign Affairs to document administrative control of the Apartheid Appropriation funds. In addition, WUS acquired funding and the Apartheid Committee got access to necessary contacts, documentation and useful channels.

The political nature of Andersen's expansion: Limits for change

The double-sided nature of the Apartheid Appropriation, serving both a humanitarian and a political purpose, remained in place after the expansion in volume. The Apartheid Appropriation had never been 'un-political'. In fact it had been created as a political response to events in South Africa in the 1960s, and there was wide consensus that Denmark should contribute with humanitarian support and advocate such support in a way that gave it maximum international bearing, in the UN and on the individual regimes. But, supporting the national liberation movements was the borderland of Danish support. Poul Hartling had supported an MPLA ambulance and education in exile, because it fitted what administratively was considered 'humanitarian' assistance. Technically this was an innovation, but it was not combined with any public profiling. Therefore, it had not been subject to any political controversy.

Under K. B. Andersen the Danish support developed differently. He did not change it technically—but increased its volume and changed its title. He included it in Denmark's international profile and, thus, made a political manifestation out of it.

---

1. Interview with Sidelmann, 3 December 1996. Minutes from Apartheid Committee meeting 2 April 1974, no date. MFA 6.U.566.a.

Going further would not have been possible for Andersen and for the Social Democratic minority government, had they wished to. Andersen's first announcements, such as his November 1971 press conference, indicate that he considered funding the liberation movements more directly. But in parliament and among the public there was no majority for such a politicised support, which would have meant a breach with Denmark's principles of working for 'peaceful conflict resolution through negotiations'. Supporting liberation movements with cash for their general running costs, or diplomatically supporting armed struggles was not politically possible for Denmark. The liberation movements often sported dogmatic Marxist rhetoric similar to that of the Soviet Union and other opponents of the Danish alliance in cold war Europe. On the other hand, there is no doubt about the political and popular humanitarian consensus in Denmark against racism and colonialism, and the support for alleviating and—to some extent—preventing the devastating economic and humanitarian consequences of these systems. In parliament, even K. B. Andersen's critics agreed with this.

The role of K. B. Andersen's political expansion in 1971/72 of the Apartheid Appropriation should, however, not be underestimated. Contemporary understanding in the public debate, even among politicians, administrators and NGOs, was that 'liberation movements could now be supported'. Even if the 'substance and practice' of the appropriation did not change, both supporters and adversaries of Andersen's policy conceptualised the debate in terms of being 'for or against the support of liberation movements'. This illustrates that K. B. Andersen's contribution in developing Denmark's role towards Southern Africa is significant. He created a political profile for Danish humanitarian support, and gave it the maximum international effect possible on the regimes responsible for racist and colonialist oppression in the region.

Chapter 4

1974: Political Struggle and Stalemate

Internationally as well as domestically, K. B. Andersen politicised the Apartheid Appropriation. South African politicians and newspapers even believed for a time that all Danish development aid would now go to 'guerrilla movements'. Presidents Julius Nyerere of Tanzania and Kenneth Kaunda of Zambia, whom Andersen had visited in March 1972, probably knew better, but praised Denmark for making a clever and righteous move. Similar reactions came from the UN Apartheid Committee. Denmark made friends.[1]

But domestically, the political expansion of the Apartheid Appropriation was heavily criticised. It was commonly believed that Denmark, through Andersen's expansion in 1972/73, had started to fund national liberation movements directly. Andersen's critics argued that these movements were communist terrorists, receiving arms from the Soviet Union to attack legal institutions in sovereign foreign states. Few other than the Ministry of Foreign Affairs and the organizations involved in the Apartheid Committee knew how to analyse the administrative technicalities, and K. B. Andersen continued to add to the confusion by repeatedly saying 'support *to* liberation movements' in his statements to the Danish press. But the practice remained the same: aid was still administered by the international and Danish NGOs in control of cash, purchases and decisions; they remained the accountable parties vis-à-vis the Danish Ministry of Foreign Affairs. And the substance of Danish support remained humanitarian, though the activities now sometimes took place on the initiative and in cooperation with national liberation movements.

In public and in parliamentary debates the practical and ideological sides of the Apartheid Appropriation were mixed up. This problem perpetuated itself even when Andersen's critics came to power in 1974, and set out to roll back Andersen's expansion.

Continued growth of the Apartheid Appropriation

From DKK 6.5 million in 1972/73, the Apartheid Appropriation was increased to DKK 8,45 million in the annual government budget for 1973/74 (April to March). The Apartheid Committee held its seasonal meetings in May and July 1973 and recommended that the bulk of the allocation (DKK 5.656 million) should go to previously supported organizations: IDAF, IUEF and WUS-International educational programmes. In addition, the UN Trust and Education

1. See Chapter 3.

Funds and the Mozambique Institute in Dar-es-Salaam received funding from the appropriation. In terms of administrative practice this was new. Since 1967, support to the UN funds and to the Institute had been given as regular development aid through Danida (or its predecessor TS).[1] Another new item was the funding of WUS-Denmark for a food aid and transport project involving Angolan refugees in MPLA camps in Zambia. The recommendations were forwarded unchanged to the standing Financial Com-mittee in Parliament, as the Minister's appropriation application. The application was approved on August 20.[2]

Simultaneously, it was learned that DKK 1.7 million allocated to the ongoing WUS-Denmark/MPLA school construction project in Dolisie, Congo (see Chapter 3) would have to be postponed to the following year.[3] This meant that DKK 1.09 million had not yet been allocated by the end of the financial year. How this money should be used was discussed at two meetings of the Apartheid Committee on October 1 and November 13, 1973. A number of applications were approved. The major beneficiaries were the South African Students' Organization (SASO) through IUEF and WUS-International, an extra grant to the WUS-Denmark/MPLA school at Dolisie to construct more buildings, and to IDAF and FNLA in Angola.[4]

The FNLA application was the most controversial and the committee discussed it quite extensively. FNLA had so far not been funded by Denmark. However, the organization had recently been recognised by the OAU, an important prerequisite for Danish assistance, in connection with attempts by Tanzania and other African countries to unite the Angolan liberation movements MPLA and FNLA. In December 1971, FNLA leader Holden Roberto had visited Denmark and the Ministry of Foreign Affairs and in 1972 the organization forwarded a rather vague application for financial support that was later refused.[5] The Danish Ambassador to Zaire however visited FNLA in 1973 and recommended support to FNLA and the Ministry invited the move-

1. See Chapter 2.
2. Appropriation Application no. 629 of 9 August 1973. 'Finansudvalgets Aktstykker' 1972/73. Note, no date, August 1973, on Financial Committee approval. MFA 6.U.566.
3. Minutes 9 May and 19 July 1973 from meetings of the Apartheid Committee the same days. MFA 6.U.566.
4. Note, 12 October 1973 on Apartheid Committee allocation recommendations made on 1 October. MFA 6.U.566. Minutes 15 October and 5 November 1973 from meetings in the Apartheid Committee, 1 October and 13 November 1973. MFA 6.U.566.a.
5. Notes, 10 December and 22 December 1971 on visits to Danida and to the political department P.3. of FNLA delegation (president Holden Roberto, Nordic Representative Mateus Neto, Henddrick Vall Neto, Samuel Abrigada, Xavier Lubota. FNLA described their positions in Angola, their refugee camps, school and health facilities in Zaire and asked for humanitarian assistance. Dispatch 24 March 1972 from Danish embassy in Zaire to the Ministry with attached FNLA 'Angola Development Plan 1972–75, Projects Searching for Aid' handed over by Holden Roberto to the Danish Ambassador in Kinshasa during a visit to the embassy the same day. Message 3 July 1972 to the embassy to inform FNLA that its requests could not been met in want of a specific application. MFA 6.U.566/11.

ment to produce a more detailed application for school equipment, which they did in September 1973.[1]

WUS was not happy about supporting FNLA. During the 'Afrika-71' campaign they had tried to contact them, but received no response. In their view, Holden Roberto and his delegation had not made a good impression during their visit to Copenhagen in 1971, using expensive hotels and rented cars, while MPLA Representative Lúcio Lara had been happy with the local bus.[2] WUS and other Apartheid Committee members argued that FNLA did not allow visitors to their liberated areas, and they felt uncertain about who the organization actually represented and if the civil activities it carried out on the ground had any significant volume.

Ministry officials argued that OAU recognition, together with UN Security Council Resolutions, formed the basis for Danish support. The Apartheid Appropriation was supposed to be a politically neutral, humanitarian facility and supporting only MPLA could be seen as political side-taking by Denmark now that the formal situation of the two movements was the same. All the NGO members recognised that FNLA met the formalities, and in the end the Ministry officials' reasoning was accepted. It was agreed to recommend an allocation of DKK 100,000 to FNLA. [3]

New government

At the time of these meetings Denmark was preparing for general elections on December 4. This interrupted the regular Apartheid Committee routine, as a new parliament had to be formed before the recommendations of the Apartheid Committee could be used for an application to the Standing Financial Committee to release the money, whether by K. B. Andersen or someone else.[4]

The elections turned the Danish political landscape upside down and produced a parliament representing ten different parties, five of them new. The Liberal Party (Venstre) formed a weak minority government, and on December 19 Prime Minister Poul Hartling and Minister of Foreign Affairs Ove Guldberg took office. The government was supported only by two minor parties, the Centre Democrats (Centrum-Demokraterne) and Christian People's Party

---

1. Note 31 August 1973: Meeting in the Ministry between Danish Ambassador to Zaire and Danida. The ambassador estimated the number of FNLA refugees in Zaire to be 400.000, and found the facts that Roberto was meant to be president of a united FNLA and MPLA, the recent recognition by Tanzania in that connection, plus the backing from Zaire as signs that FNLA was becoming the dominant Angolan liberation movement should the FNLA/MPLA cooperation fail to be indicators of FNLA's importance. He recommended Denmark support not only MPLA. Application, 27 September 1973 from FNLA. Note 19 September 1973: Request to UNHCR that found FNLA as worthy of Danish support as MPLA. MFA 6.U.566/11.
2. Interview with Peder Sidelmann, 3 December 1996.
3. See note 4 on previous page.
4. Note 28 November 1973 describing how the Apartheid Committee recommendations of 1 October and 13 November had to await elections and the forming of a new government and standing financial committee. MFA 6.U.566.

(Kristeligt Folkeparti), and its power base was mainly that other parties had not been able to produce a different majority coalition.

Along with the right wing Conservative Party (Konservative Folkeparti), Venstre had led the opposition in the former parliament, and had fronted the criticism of K. B. Andersen's expansion of the Apartheid Appropriation and the Apartheid Committee. Now, Ove Guldberg inherited the Apartheid Appropriation, the Apartheid Committee, and the question of how to distribute the remaining DKK 1 million of the 1973/74 allocation. Previously, Venstre and Konservative had often voted against the allocations in the Standing Financial Committee. However, when the major part of the 1973/74 allocation had been approved before the elections in August 1973, they had abstained. This had been interpreted internally in the Ministry of Foreign Affairs as a sign of the expanded Apartheid Appropriation having become less controversial.

To brief the new Minister, the Ministry produced a memorandum on the background, size and practices of the Apartheid Appropriation.[1] They listed the 'established guidelines due to political circumstances' for the appropriation to be as follows:

— the allocations are not subject to any geographical restrictions, but UN Security Council Resolutions on Southern Africa, to secure that the UN Charter principle of non-interference is not violated, in practice restrict support to the Southern African region,
— Denmark's overall principle is that conflicts should be solved through negotiations rather than armed struggle. This prescribes that national liberation movements do not receive support in cash that may be used for buying arms,
— Denmark does not choose between rivalling liberation movements in an area, but uses recognition by the OAU as a prerequisite for support,
— a neighbouring host or transit country must accept the passing of Danish support through its territory, and
— supporting a liberation movement does not mean recognition of that movement in terms of international law.[2]

The memo also specified the activities supported in the current financial year (the DKK 5.656 million already allocated, plus the 1.7 million set aside for the WUS/MPLA Dolisie school) and provided the recommendations the Apartheid Committee had made for the remaining one million in October/November. The technical budgeting details, like the reshuffle between the financial years, were

1. The change of government was an occasion to describe and define practices of the Apartheid Appropriation, as by-laws or formal statutes had never been produced. The closest to a 'founding document' was Minister of Foreign Affairs Per Hækkerup's first Appropriation Application to the Standing Financial Committee in 1965. See Chapter 3.
2. Memorandum 18 December 1973 summing up practices, political background and current status of the Apartheid Appropriation and the Apartheid Committee. MFA 6.U.566.

explained, as they were in each of the appropriation applications to the standing Financial Committee.

A different conclusion

In January 1974, Ove Guldberg revealed his views on how funds should be allocated. He—'the new government'—was not against 'educational and humanitarian aid to oppressed peoples or groups who are victims of apartheid'.[1] This formulation is a copy of the Apartheid Appropriation title and signals that Guldberg did not question the existence of the appropriation: 'Such assistance was also practised by the Right/Liberal coalition government of 1968–71', he continued and stated no plans to reduce the appropriation. The government was, however, concerned with how the funds were utilized and if there was sufficient control to prevent misuse. Guldberg emphasised that the appropriation should not function as assistance to national liberation movements, but provide educational and humanitarian aid to the victims of apartheid. He did not feel confident that the liberation movements spent existing funds in ways that Denmark could approve of, and he therefore preferred the remaining DKK one million to be paid as an advance instalment to IDAF, as he trusted an international organization to be more accountable.

On the basis of the mentioned Ministry memo of December 18, Guldberg's decisions are interesting. The document outlined how Denmark had never provided cash support and it specified what educational and humanitarian activities were carried out by which NGO, whether they worked independently, through their international networks or with a national liberation movement. Part of the reason why Guldberg wanted a change of practice anyway, may be found in the continued confusion of the 'to' or 'through' debate (as discussed in Chapter 3). When K. B. Andersen expanded the Apartheid Appropriation it was announced—also by Andersen himself—that funds might now also go *to* national liberation movements. However, when he amended the title of the Apartheid Appropriation, it was with the phrase '... or *through* liberation movements'. When allocations started, the practice was yet more indirect: through NGOs that in some cases cooperated with a liberation movement. This was clearly explained in the December 18 memo.

If Guldberg actually did fear that Danish funds were distributed 'to' the movements, he must have suspected that Danish NGOs deliberately misused funds. Apparently, he did not suspect this to apply to international organizations like IDAF. Yet, the Danish control of organizations like IDAF or IUEF was weaker than the control of the Danish NGOs involved. IDAF pooled their funds from different donors, and substantial sums, for legal aid and maintenance for families of detainees etc, were more or less secretly sent into South Africa. IDAF had been banned in South Africa since 1966 and to a large extent

---

1. Note 15 February 1974 referring to the extraordinary Apartheid Committee meeting 12 February where Guldberg's views were communicated to the committee. MFA.6.U.566.

K. B. Andersen and Minister of Foreign
Affairs, Ove Guldberg, disagreeing on
Danish support to MPLA, February 1974.
(Photo: Scanpix/Willy Lund)

had to rely on personal relations. Consequently it was very hard to audit IDAF
in a traditional manner.

Guldberg however never mentioned any indications of misuse by Danish
NGOs nor did he give any specific reasons for suspicion. Thus, the motive for
his hostility, which neither reduced or abolished the appropriation, nor dissolved or changed the Apartheid Committee, seems unclear and will be discussed below.

Guldberg's policy was communicated to the Apartheid Committee at an
extraordinary meeting on February 12, 1974. The Committee regretted that
their original recommendations would not be accepted, but suggested a compromise leaving about DKK 500,000 for IDAF, while the rest of the surplus
million would be allocated to projects it was considered would suffer severely
from a halt in the support. However, a week later Guldberg decided that all of
the remaining money would be forwarded to IDAF. Apart from the fact that it
would now become harder to control and verify the use of the money, another
consequence was that the grant to FNLA, which the Ministry administration
had argued hard to have included, was cancelled.[1]

---

1. Ibid. with continuation 20 February 1974 that Guldberg the same day had decided to grant all
   of the remaining DKK one milllion to IDAF. Minutes 13 March 1974 from extraordinary meeting 12 February of the Apartheid Committee. MFA 6.U.566.a. The allocations that the Apartheid Committee wished to maintain were: IUEF information and training in South Africa, WUS-
   I slum health education in South Africa and WUS-DK construction of extension at MPLA school
   in Dolisie, Congo.

NGOs concerned, but not alarmed

On March 20, the Standing Financial Committee in parliament approved Guld-berg's appropriation application allocating all the money to IDAF. The formal application mentions that the Apartheid Committee had recommended a diffe-ent use of the funds, but that the Committee had approved the changes.[1]

There are no indications that the Apartheid Committee did actually approve of this deviation from its own recommendations. At the meeting in February 1974, the Committee had disagreed with Guldberg's plans and pro-posed a compromise. On March 16, the Committee repeated its regrets in a let-ter to Guldberg explaining that it had always made consensus decisions and that previous Foreign Ministers had always approved its former recommenda-tions.[2]

It is remarkable that this is the Apartheid Committee's only reaction. For the first time the Committee had been over-ruled. At their next meeting, on April 2, no comments were made and no concerns expressed. At this point, the Committee might not have taken Guldberg's position too seriously, since no specific allegations had been made of misuse of funds, and because the Minister had chosen to let IDAF receive the money.[3]

Next year's applications were discussed and some of them recommended to the Minister. Apart from some minor changes, the list was an update of the Committee's recommendations the previous year. The newcomers were a World Council of Churches (WCC) agricultural programme for food aid to Angolan refugees, OAU food, health and educational programmes for the Angolan and Mozambiquan Movements (including FNLA) and the UN fund for the planned Namibia Institute in Zambia.[4]

The political parties supporting the Apartheid Appropriation in its existing form did not react to Ove Guldberg's initiative either. Almost all parties repre-sented on the Standing Financial Committee, including the Social Democratic Party, voted for Guldberg's choice of granting IDAF the remaining million. Even K. B. Andersen, now a central figure in the opposition, did not react, and the incident is not mentioned in his memoirs.

One reason may be that the new government inherited the national budget for 1974/75 from the previous Social Democratic government and accepted the built-in increase in the volume of the Apartheid Appropriation, from DKK 8.45 million to 12.4 million. The new government must have known that a

---

1. Appropriation Application no. 226, 11 March 1974. Finansudvalgets Aktstykker 1973/74.
2. Letter 16 March 1974 from NGO members of the Apartheid Committee accompanying pam-phlet produced by the NGOs describing support funded by the Apartheid Appropriation. The letter is an implicit reference to the Right-Liberal coalition government of 1968–71, where the current Prime Minister Poul Hartling served as Minister of Foreign Affairs. MFA 6.U.566.
3. None of the interviewed Apartheid Committee members or administrators of activities funded by the Apartheid Appropriation remember having any reason to suspect that the overruling of the Apartheid Committee was more than a one time incident. For instance, Max Kruse 14 Janu-ary 1997, Arne Piel Christensen 14 May 1997 and Peder Sidelmann 3 December 1996.
4. Minutes (no date) of meeting of the Apartheid Committee 2 April 1974. MFA 6.U.566.a.

majority in parliament would have voted against a reduction, since the increase was mainly the result of previous multi-lateral development assistance being integrated into the Apartheid Appropriation, such as some IUEF and WUS scholarship programmes for refugees in neighbouring countries.[1]

Initiatives for public action

While Ove Guldberg and the Apartheid Committee started their tug of war about how Danish official funds should be allocated, NGOs outside the Apartheid Committee worked to mobilise public attention and debate on Southern Africa. In comparison to the Vietnam movement, the NGO and grass roots initiatives seeking to focus the political and public debate on Southern Africa were few and involved few people. Their background was church based and/or springing from the 'New Left' student movement.

When the World Council of Churches (WCC) established its 'Programme to Combat Racism' (PCR) in 1968/69 it also launched a 'Special Support Fund' in collaboration with national liberation movements, and invited individual member churches to contribute.[2] DanChurchAid (DCA) set aside funds for this purpose, but the board, in order 'not to confuse humanitarian and political support', had withdrawn the allocation.[3] During 1971 the church community discussed plans to establish a Danish branch of PCR, but it was still considered controversial for established church based organizations to support liberation movements. Instead, 'Kirkernes Raceprogram' (KR) was launched at the beginning of 1972 as an independent organization.[4]

The founders and activists of KR came from a small group of theology and political science students and young graduates at the University of Århus. The conscientious objector Leif Vestergaard was assigned the responsibility for KR by Århus Ecumenical Centre, which also provided the facilities for the organization and continued to fund Vestergaard part time from 1972–74. KR's main activity was information and it produced a presentation folder, a poster and a booklet on racism from a theological perspective. In connection with a major scout jamboree, KR distributed a pamphlet on racism, living conditions and liberation movements in Southern Africa, and arranged a poster exhibition. KR also gave lectures in local church communities, held a seminar for church and youth leaders, and hosted visits by the Namibian Anglican Bishop in exile Colin Winter, Head of PCR Baldwin Sjollema and WCC General Secretary

---

1. Folketingets Forhandlinger 1973/74, F1113 and D1 (1st session); F 4374, D553 and B4 (2nd session). Minutes, 13 March 1974. MFA 6.U.566.a.
2. See Chapter 3.
3. The 'Special Fund' allocated in 1970 and 1971 funds to all the major national liberation movements in Southern Africa (including FNLA, UNITA, ZAPU and ZANU), to PAIGC and to non-racist organizations in the Americas and Asia. Support was given to humanitarian and educational activities and explicitly without any control measures.
4. Kirkernes Raceprogram, annual report Jan 1972–Feb 1973. LV. Memorandum by Langhoff, no date, on the launch of KR and its background. KR. Interview with Leif Vestergaard, April 1996.

Philip Potter. In its first year KR raised DKK 30,000. The money went to the WCC's 'Special Fund' and was administrated by the Copenhagen Diocese.[1]

WCC recommended sanctions against South Africa, and KR also started to focus on trade. In March 1974 a report called 'Danmarks aktier i [shares in] Apartheid & Co' was published—a detailed documentation of Danish business involvement in South Africa. A lot of the material was collected by KR member Jørgen Lissner, who had travelled under cover in South Africa and met with trade unionists. More information was collected in Danish business registers etc.[2]

Through Lissner's local trade union connections, KR discovered that the Durban branch of the major Danish trading company 'East Asian Company' (EAC) paid even lower wages than the official South African minimum. KR members started to buy individual shares in EAC, which gave them the right to speak at the company's annual General Meeting, held on March 27. For two whole hours, a group of 'shareholders', amongst them Bishop Torkild Græsholt, managed to direct the attention of the one-day Assembly to EAC's activities in South Africa. They suggested reforms, abolition of 'starvation wages', better conditions for the workers and negotiations with trade unions. A counter-motion from the EAC board stopped the discussion, but in the course of the next 9 months, the wages were raised by 30 per cent. The event was widely covered by the press, and attention was also drawn to EAC and other Danish companies violating UN sanctions on Rhodesia from 1968. The Public Prosecutor started to investigate the EAC branch in Salisbury, but no charges were filed. The branch was technically not violating sanctions, as it was neither into international transactions nor transferred funds to or from the main office in Denmark.

In the following years similar actions were carried out at every EAC General Assembly, now requesting EAC to withdraw from and boycott South Africa. This escalation started after the South African Council of Churches (SACC) encouraged KR to start working for sanctions.[3] In 1972 the WCC asked its member churches to pressure national businesses to give up investment in South Africa, and in 1973 it had published a pamphlet: 'Time to Withdraw—Investments in Southern Africa'. It was, however, fundamental for KR that its actions should be based on direct information and recommendations from church and other contacts inside South Africa.[4]

After having included sanctions in its policy, KR started picketing against South African commodities in shops, at the wholesale vegetable market etc. As a variant, individual members of KR got themselves elected to the boards of

1. Kirkernes Raceprogram, annual report Jan 1972–Feb 1973. LV.
2. Kirkernes Raceprogram: 'Danmarks Aktier i Apartheid og Co', 1974. Interview with Max Kruse, 14 January 1997.
3. *Politiken*, 8, 9, 19, 21 and 28 March and 10 and 13 April 1974, 23 March 1975, *Kristeligt Dagblad*, 1 April 1977, *Ekstra Bladet*, 1 April 1978. Knudsen, 1989.
4. Conversation with Leif Vestergaard, April 1996.

several branches of the cooperative supermarket 'Brugsen', the biggest Danish chain of supermarkets. They convinced members of local branches, and later a majority at the national Brugsen Annual General Meeting, to stop selling South African commodities. Through picketing and information activities KR was also successful in stopping the supermarket chains 'Irma' and 'Dansk Supermarket' from selling South African products. Through its information work, lectures in local parishes and in the church network, KR was a successful campaigner in parts of the Danish society that were otherwise not in contact with solidarity work.[1]

After a visit of the international 'Namibian Caravan' in Denmark, from October 9–12, 1973, a handful of the Danish activists established 'Aktionsgruppen Namibia' ('The Namibia Group') to inform about the political and humanitarian consequences of the South African occupation. The Caravan had toured Europe in October and November 1973 to inform about the political and social conditions in Namibia and to appeal for Western involvement on the basis of Namibia's status as a UN Trusteeship. In Copenhagen, an ad hoc group of small NGOs arranged street theatre, a public meeting, a press conference and a meeting with Minister of Foreign Affairs K. B. Andersen and in Århus KR had coordinated a similar programme.[2]

From the very beginning the Namibia Group focused on the Danish Fur Centre Auctions, the Northern Europe trading centre for the important Namibian export item, 'Swakara' pelts. At the annual exhibition and auctions of the Danish Fur Breeders Association in February and March 1974, the campaigners put up a four-panel exhibition board and handed out information leaflets at the entrance of the exhibition hall, based on a report the Namibia Group had made about the Danish fur trade. A press conference was held at the exhibition with the participation of Ben Amathila, the SWAPO representative to the Nordic countries and Germany, and Ove Jensen, a local MP and member of the board of the Danish Fur Centre.[3]

The Namibia Action Group continued its activities after its action against Swakara fur sales. As a follow up of the detention of ten SWAPO leaders in February 1974, the group distributed postcards for individuals to send to Prime Minister John Vorster requiring the release of the SWAPO leaders, and other political prisoners. By the end of March it hosted a new visit by SWAPO

1. Interview with Max Kruse, 14 January 1997.
2. The 'Namibia Caravan' was an international group of people based at the 'European Work Group', Gross Heere, West Germany. It visited ten countries with the caravan. After the tour it became the 'Namibia Transnational Collective. Namibia Caravan Report—October-November. 29 January 1974. KG.
3. Open letter 21 February 1974 from the Namibia Group to Danish Fur Centre Auctions. Namibia Group presentation pamphlet, 25 February 1974. KG. Demokraten 25 February 1974. Talk with Kirsten Gauffriau, 18 March 1997.

Representative Ben Amathila and organized meetings with the press and with press and with political parties, including former Minister Andersen.[1]

When UN Commissioner to Namibia, Sean McBride, visited Denmark in May 1974, to meet with Minister of Foreign Affairs, Ove Guldberg, representatives of the Danish Parliament and the Danish government, the Namibia Group arranged a public meeting at the 'Ecumenical Centre' where McBride informed about Namibia. The group also helped to arrange a TV-interview on national television, led by journalist and Social Democratic MP, Lasse Budtz. And in May, the Namibia Group met with the standing Foreign Policy Committee in Parliament (Folketingets Udenrigsudvalg). Here, it presented a paper recommending Denmark to become member of the UN council for Namibia, to contribute financially to the UN Institute for Namibia in Lusaka, to officially support SWAPO and officially condemn the harassment of SWAPO in Namibia. It is interesting to note that these requirements, which were based on McBride and SWAPO information, did not include sanctions but were limited to a call for more indirect support of SWAPO and diplomatic pressure.[2]

Later in 1974, the Namibia Action Group played an active role in establishing a working partnership with a variety of political and church organizations, to organize a 'Namibia-75 Campaign'. This was an information campaign aimed at the Danish public about political and social conditions in Namibia, a fund raising campaign for SWAPO refugee camps in Zambia, for the 'Black Educational Association' and cooperation between SWAPO and church organizations in Namibia. A 'Namibia Seminar' was held on 8–9 February 1975 with the participation of Ben Amathila from SWAPO and Peter Jones from the International Fellowship of Reconciliation (IFOR).[3]

Pressure from the right

When Ove Guldberg's initiative to maintain the volume but change the channels of the Apartheid Appropriation was finally challenged, the reaction did not come from the supporters of the Appropriation. The critic was the ultra right wing newcomer 'Fremskridtspartiet', a populist party that for the first time had entered parliament on promises of tax reductions and budget cuts.

---

1. Invitation from the Namibia Action Group to political parties 24 March 1974. Press statement 27 March 1974. Printed postcard to Prime Minister Vorster April 1974.
2. Letter 14 May 1974 from Namibia Action Group to Lasse Budtz, Danish Broadcasting. Requests 29 May 1974 from the Namibia Group to Parliament, presented during an interview with the Standing Foreign Committee the same day. KG.
3. Among the participating organizations were the students' 'Trinitatis' parish, IFOR-Denmark, the Danish Communist Party, the Liberal Party's Youth Organization (VU), the Danish Youth Council and individuals e.g. Knud Erik Rosenkrantz from WUS. Namibia-75 presentation letter 2 May 1975. Minutes, no date, from seminar 8–9 February 1975. KG. The campaign was financed with funds from member organizations and from Danida's information funds. At first, the applications were turned down, but through direct correspondence with K.B Andersen the money was granted in January 1975 after he became Minister of Foreign Affairs again. Letter 29 January 1975 from Andersen to Kirsten Gauffriau of Namibia Action Group. KG.

Fremskridtspartiet was the second biggest party and fiercely opposed to development assistance. It was the only party voting against Guldberg's IDAF allocation in the Finance Committee in March, and in a parliamentary question hour in April, Fremskridtspartiet's Holger Lindholt asked Guldberg if the Minister could guarantee that funds from the Apartheid Appropriation went to humanitarian and educational aid and not to military purposes.[1]

The question was based on a special edition in the magazine 'Sydafrika Kontakt' on Angolan partners of the 'Afrika-71' campaign. Among the articles was one by WUS-activist and Campaign Coordinator Peder Sidelmann on MPLA's educational strategies. He quoted an MPLA policy paper on how academic and practical skills 'were combined in the education, to link it to the revolutionary process and to production... Therefore, education will include training in the use of arms in the defence of villages and in the principles of revolutionary organization, next to mathematics, physics, history etc.'[2] The paragraph followed a description of the plans for two MPLA schools in exile in Congo and in Zambia, the former being the WUS school project in Dolisie.

Guldberg replied on April 24. He said that Apartheid Appropriation funds were allocated exclusively for humanitarian and educational purposes, in accordance with UN and OAU directions and with no payments in cash to liberation movements. In the debate that followed, Lindholt referred to Sidelmann's article—which was not mentioned in his question nor in its motivation—as proof of Danish funds being used for guerrilla training. He further indicated that WUS financial reporting was incomplete, making it possible to misuse funds for military purposes. Apparently, Guldberg was not prepared to discuss Sidelmann's article and he merely repeated the existing principles and technicalities concerning the administration of the appropriation. Further, he made clear that nothing was missing in the financial reporting, but that he would continue to see to it in the future.[3]

Apart from Guldberg and Lindholt, the only other MP who participated in the debate was Bent Honoré from Christian People's Party (Kristeligt Folkeparti), one of the two minor parties that supported the Venstre government. Honoré urged Guldberg to inform parliament about any missing reporting, as he saw this as a crucial point in the debate. Guldberg promised to do so, but he did not mention anything about his own critical attitude towards the appropriation. It is interesting how Guldberg responded in a very similar manner to the way K. B. Andersen had done.

Holger Lindholt's question drew some public attention and newspapers began to write about how the Apartheid Appropriation had been increased in

1. Note 17 April 1974: Question to Minister Guldberg by Lindholt, with text of Guldberg's answer. MFA 6.U.566.
2. *Sydafrika Kontakt*, No 3, 1972.
3. Question to Minister of Foreign Affairs by Linholdt, debated in Parliament 24 April 1974. Folketingets Forhandlinger 1973/74, F 5474 to 5478.

the new budget. The following day, Sidelmann explained in an interview that the MPLA policy paper quoted by Lindholt applied to schools in liberated areas within Angola, in order to defend them from Portuguese attacks. No such training took place at the Dolisie secondary school in Congo. Although it was clear from the article that Sidelmann referred to an MPLA report about its education policies in general, he had not specified that Dolisie was an exception as regards the clause on military training. Lindholt, in a letter to the editor, rejected Sidelmann's interview statement and maintained that the quote from the article proved that Dolisie conducted military training.[1]

Guldberg suspicious of the Apartheid Appropriation

In June 1974, Ove Guldberg informed the Ministry that he wished to change the practice of the Apartheid Appropriation funds being channelled through private organizations. He disapproved of the role played by the organizations involved that 'seemed to be infected by people with certain political standpoints'. He found that 'they had a tendency of multiplying into chains of institutions which made the aid still more indirect'. Guldberg concluded that he wanted to do away with these arrangements, and with the Danish administration of individual projects. He preferred using multilateral organizations such as the UN. It did not trouble him that one effect of this move would be to end Danish support to education, legal aid and social programmes inside South Africa, Namibia, Rhodesia and the Portuguese colonies. Support would be restricted to Southern Africans in exile, since the UN could not work inside countries where the formally recognised governments did not allow it.[2]

The Ministry started to work on this change of policy. Telegrams were dispatched to Danish representations at, or near, UN headquarters, to inquire whether FAO, UNESCO, UNHCR or the special UN programmes for Southern Africa could handle increased funds. UNHCR, the UN Trust Fund and the UN Educational and Training Programme replied positively. The UNHCR could work with the national liberation movements in exile, but it was emphasised that the UN Educational Programme could not take over support to scholarships inside the territories. The Ministry went through the previous year's allocations and the current year's Apartheid Committee recommendations from April, to analyse which activities would be able to continue with funding through UN bodies, and which would not. The change of policy would mainly affect the scholarships and social programmes within the territories, whereas

---

1. *Politiken,* 25 April and 1 May 1974.
2. Note, 17 June 1974 referring to Guldberg's scepticism of NGOs as channels for Danish official funds and intentions to channel all funds through the UN. MFA 6.U.566.

support to Frelimo, MPLA, FNLA and PAIGC educational and social activities could continue to receive Danish funds through the relevant UN bodies.[1]

Along the new lines, the Ministry produced Appropriation Application no 435 for the Finance Committee for 1974/75, for the first time overruling the Apartheid Committee. The Finance Committee received it from the Minister on July 31. The existing UN allocations were doubled or trebled and some of the humanitarian assistance—like food, medicine, teaching equipment—were supposed to be distributed 'through liberation movements recognised by the OAU'. The usual NGO channels were no longer to be used. Some activities, not fitting the new model, were ended, whereas other activities were continued—some with reduced allocations.[2]

Formally, the proposal implied a change of channels, not of beneficiaries. 'Oppressed peoples or groups' were still mentioned in the appropriation title as the targets for allocations, and also in the motivation section of the Appropriation application. On the contrary, it specified that parts of the support should go to facilities administrated and controlled by national liberation movements.

Guldberg's initiative was not based on how the Apartheid Appropriation funds could be allocated most effectively. It is difficult to see how the use of UN administrative bodies would be 'more direct' than previous practices. The point was to get around the Danish organizations, although Guldberg never pointed to any specific example of the 'political attitude' that concerned him about the NGOs, nor examples of funds having been misused. On the other hand, he had

---

1. Note, 27 June 1974 discussing the consequences of changing the practice of Apartheid Appropriation allocations, with appendix. It was predicted that the Apartheid Committee would have a very limited role to play, but that dissolving it would lead to political criticism. The suggested increase in allocations to the UN Trust Fund from 0.6 to over 3 million would make Denmark the largest donor. MFA 6.U.566.a. Cables 2 July 1974 to missions in Rome, Paris, Geneva and New York requesting information whether FAO, UNESCO, UNHCR or the UN Programmes for Southern Africa could channel increased funding. Note, 4 July on visit the same day to the Ministry of UNHCR Director for Refugees Ole Volfing. Cable 23 August from the Danish mission to the UN that the UN education programmes could use more funds, but would not be able to channel support to within South Africa, Namibia, Zimbabwe and Portuguese colonies. The UN Trust Fund channels included IDAF and WCC, some of the organizations that Guldberg mistrusted as 'agencies'. Memorandum 5 July, final version 26 July, listing 1974/75 allocations as suggested 2 April by the Apartheid Committee with notes on what future UN channelling could support them or if support would cease. MFA 6.U.566.

2. Note, 28 June 1974 on Guldberg's approval of a new practice of allocating Apartheid Appropriation funds. MFA 6.U.566.a. The UN Trust Fund was to receive DKK 1.5 million and the Education and Training Programme 3 million compared to DKK 0.6 and 0.85 million, respectively, in 1973/74. Grants to UNHCR would be increased to DKK 3.7 million from 1.5 million and the WHO, WFP, UNICEF and UNESCO were to receive DKK 0.5 million each. To be continued were the educational programmes for refugees funded through the UN 'Education and Training Programme for Southern Africa', UNHCR and UNESCO instead of IUEF and WUS-I (including the MPLA Dolisie School for the remaining two years of construction work). The WFP and UNHCR were to become channels for food aid and equipment to refugee camps administerted by the liberation movements. Also, some legal assistance, maintenance and other social programmes inside South Africa, Rhodesia and the Portuguese colonies were continued indirectly on a reduced scale through the UN Trust Fund. The Fund—unlike other UN bodies—channelled support through international NGOs such as IDAF and WCC.

not taken into account that the new arrangement would make Denmark the dominating donor to UN funds and result in the overall turnover of these bodies increasing sharply, and possibly beyond their capacity.[1]

The initiative was also a consequence of the criticisms by Guldberg and his Liberal party against K. B. Andersen in 1972–73. The critique had been aimed at Andersen's political announcements of giving *to* the national liberation movements, rather than at the 'substance and practice' of the Apartheid Appropriation. Thus, the initiative was mainly aimed at changing the political profile of the support and Guldberg now had to manoeuvre between critics both from the Fremskridtspartiet right and the Social Democratic left side of the political landscape.

Fighting the minister

In the morning of July 26, 1974, the Apartheid Committee met and was informed about Guldberg's decision. The Committee was shocked, and expressed their 'lack of understanding for the rationale' behind the initiative.[2] In the afternoon the NGO committee members met again without the Ministry officials and produced a letter to the Minister questioning the decision. They emphasised that there had never been any reason to question how the NGOs used the funds, that the UN would not be able to take over many of the activities in Southern Africa, which consequently would have to be stopped, and that it was questionable if the UN had sufficient capacity and contacts to secure that the support reached the beneficiaries.[3]

On August 1, the same day the Standing Financial Committee received his appropriation application, Ove Guldberg expressed his intentions to change the channels for the Apartheid Appropriation in a commentary in the daily 'Politiken'.[4] He stressed how difficult it was to control funds with several minor allocations, and the subsequent risk of military misuse by the liberation movements. The supporters of the Apartheid Appropriation in its existing form then started a massive campaign against Guldberg in the press, using the same arguments against him as the Apartheid Committee had.[5] From the other side, there were right wing letters to editors that saw Sidelmann's article as documentation of Danish official funds being used for military training and held WUS responsible for this misuse. One referred to an internal report in the Ministry that allegedly documented such misuse and Fremskridtspartiet criticised Guldberg for not abolishing the Apartheid Appropriation: 'Does the increased

1. Note, 27 June 1974. MFA 6.U.566.a
2. Minutes (no date) from Apartheid Committee meeting 26 July 1974.
3. Note 26 July 1974 on meeting of the Apartheid Committee the same day. 6.U.566.a. Letter 26 July to the Minister of Foreign Affairs from Apartheid Committee members, in: Minutes, 21 August 1974. MFA 6.U.566 DanChurchAid executive meeting 12 August 1974. FKNår.
4. *Politiken*, 1 August 1974.
5. Letters to the editor, for instance: *Politiken*, 4 August, *Kristeligt Dagblad*, 6 August, *B.T.* 7 August, *Aktuelt*, 7 August, *Frederiksborg Amtsavis*, 12 August 1974.

support to Africa mean that the governing Right-Liberal party 'Venstre' had become socialist? If not, the Prime Minister had better explain.'[1]

The discussion in the Standing Finance Committee was originally scheduled for August 12, but instead the Committee declined to approve the application and requested Guldberg to explain *why* the Danish policy would need to be changed. The supporters of the Apartheid Appropriation in its existing form even convinced the Standing Foreign Committee to have Guldberg explain what in its request called 'changes of principle' in Danish foreign policy.[2]

Explanations and withdrawal

On September 13, Ove Guldberg explained to the Foreign Committee that Peder Sidelmann's article on education and military training had come to his knowledge when Holger Lindholt had asked questions in Parliament in April. Guldberg said the article had made him uncertain, although he previously had been confident that Denmark's assistance to liberation movements was never in cash. According to him, any doubts about the Apartheid Appropriation might threaten the image of all Denmark's technical and development assistance. To avoid this, he wanted to change the support channels, even though he wished to continue to support the same activities as before, including those of the liberation movements.[3]

This is a very different position from what Guldberg had communicated to the Apartheid Committee in January, and from his reasoning in the March application to the Finance Committee about transferring the remaining 1973/74 Apartheid Appropriation DKK one million to IDAF. It is the background and motivation for Guldberg's initiative that seem to be the reason for this incoherence.

Interestingly, the discussion in the Foreign Committee did not touch upon the core of Guldberg's UN alternative: that it was supposed to be more transparent than the existing procedures.

K. B. Andersen was one of the members of the Foreign Committee. Not surprisingly, he argued that public debate had fully clarified that the MPLA did not use the Dolisie school for arms training, and that Sidelmann's article had said no such thing. That aside, Andersen had no problems with arms training inside liberated areas in Angola, in order to defend schools from attacks from Portuguese forces. Secondly, Andersen asked Guldberg for documentation or examples that could justify his suspicion against the NGOs. He referred to a discussion in June in the Foreign Committee where Guldberg had described

---

1. For instance: *B.T.* 13, 21 and 27 August 1974. There is no report or references to a report documenting WUS misuse of funds in Ministry files, and it is not mentioned by Guldberg as support for his proposed change of practice for the Apartheid Appropriation.
2. Request 12 August from the Standing Parliamentary Financial Committee to Minister of Foreign Affairs for further motivation for a change of practice in allocating the Apartheid Appropriation. MFA 6.U.566.
3. Internal minutes made by Danida from a meeting of the Parliamentary Foreign Policy Committee, 13 September 1974. MFA 6.U.566.

WUS in positive terms, quoting the Danish Ambassador to Zaire who visited Dolisie in July 1973 and April 1974. His reports had been very enthusiastic about the concept of the project, the progress made and the general results. K. B. Andersen also referred to recent audits of the WUS office in Copenhagen as well as Dolisie, showing that no misuse had taken place.[1]

Finally, K. B. Andersen felt that Guldberg should have discussed his urge to change the procedures with the Foreign Committee before submitting his appropriation application to the Finance Committee. He said that the application which 'no longer meant supporting national liberation movements directly represented a fundamental change in Danish foreign policy'. But on this point, Andersen was either mistaken or polemic. Guldberg's initiative would not reduce the directness of the support, as funds had not been given 'to' the movements anyway (see Chapter 3).

The Kristeligt Folkeparti representative Bent Honoré, member of the Foreign Committee as well as the Finance Committee, found that 'it was time for other solutions than the one Guldberg had suggested'. He recognised that Guldberg had been concerned about Sidelmann's article, but found that there was no evidence to support that military training took place at Dolisie.

The meeting ended with Guldberg promising to forward documentation about eventual misuse of funds channelled through NGOs, plus a copy of the Apartheid Committee's recommendations and the reports from the Ambassador to Zaire. Only the latter were sent, along with a note from Guldberg repeating that his initiative did not include any fundamental change of Danish policy but was solely a matter of changing the channels. This was the same response as he had given to the Financial Committee in August.[2]

An interesting point is that Guldberg never made any real efforts to convince Bent Honoré about the possibility of misuse. Kristeligt Folkeparti was one of the two minor parties that had pledged support to the fragile minority government, and Honoré held the decisive vote on both the Finance and the Foreign Committees. Guldberg should have been prepared for Honorés scepticism. Honoré had contacted him in July, explaining that he had personally investigated the allegations forwarded by Holger Lindholdt in April. Honoré had read audit reports and he had met with Klaus Wulff from WUS and Johannes Langhoff from the diocese of Copenhagen, representing the Danish Programme to Combat Racism (Kirkernes Raceprogram) in the Apartheid Committee. This had convinced him that no money had been spent for arms purchases and that no military training took place at Dolisie. In his answering letter, Ove Guldberg maintained his general views on the difficulties involved in controlling and auditing the use of the funds. He also expressed doubts about

---

1. Ibid. The Ambassador's reports from visits to Dolisie, 3 August 1973 and 30 April 1974. Also filed under September 1974. MFA 6.U.566. Reports on audit control of WUS' Dolisie project 31 August in Congo and in Denmark 2 September 1974. WUS 16.4.
2. Memo, no date, with response to the Standing Financial Committee's request of 12 August 1974. MFA 6.U.566.

Wulff and Langhoff being able to guarantee that no misuse took place. But Guldberg never made any real efforts to address Honoré's clear concerns.[1]

On September 20, the Finance Committee met again to consider the appropriation application. It soon became clear that a majority wanted to turn down the application. Only the right wing parties supported it, whereas the Social Democratic Party reiterated its criticism of Guldberg's initiative, followed by the left wing and centre parties. Honoré repeated that he was still not convinced about the alleged risks of misuse, as no documentation had been presented to him. This being the central point in the Minister's rationale for changing practices, Honoré's conclusion was to maintain his vote against the application. The Finance Committee refused it, and recommended the Minister to continue allocating funds according to existing practices.[2]

By the beginning of October, the Ministry drafted a second application to the Finance Committee, this time largely following the recommendations made by the Apartheid Committee in April. Interestingly, it was conveyed to K. B. Andersen who had led the opposition against Minister Guldberg. After discussing it with Arbejderbevægelsens Solidaritetsfond (The Workers Solidarity Fund—see Chapter 3), WUS and the Social Democratic MPs, Andersen had a meeting with Ministry officials to give his comments. The proposal was discussed at an Apartheid Committee meeting on October 30, and not surprisingly, the Committee only had minor comments to what was basically their own proposal. The next day, the final version was sent to the Finance Committee that approved it at its next meeting on November 13. And so, the Apartheid Appropriation was back to its old lines of practice.[3]

Political positions

When K. B. Andersen had expanded the scope of the Apartheid Appropriation in 1972, it was debated and criticised, in particular by Liberals like Guldberg and Hartling as well as the Conservatives. The two main issues had been that national liberation movements were communist or dominated by communists, and that the members of the Apartheid Committee and their international contacts were predominantly socialist sympathisers.

When Guldberg took office, it would not have been surprising if he had wanted to cut the links to the liberation movements, change the composition of the Apartheid Committee, or even dissolve it. In this perspective, Guldberg's

---

1. Letter 10 July 1974 from MP Bent Honoré to the Minister of Foreign Affairs, letter 25 July 1974 from Ove Guldberg to Honoré. MFA 6.U.566. Today, Honoré remembers likewise: 'I could not see from the documents I received that the allocation was used as Guldberg feared.' Interview with Honoré 13 May 1997.
2. Note 20 September 1974 accompanying the Standing Financial Committee's rejection the same day of appropriation application no 435. MFA 6.U.566.
3. Note 8 October 1974, draft appropriation application. Minutes 28 October 1974 from meeting with K. B. Andersen discussing note 8 October. MFA 6.U.566. Minutes, no date, Apartheid Committee meeting 30 October 1974. FKNra. Appropriation Application no 58, Finansudvalgets Aktstykker 1974/75.

initiative in 1974 was remarkably low key. It did not mention the national liberation movements' possible communist affiliations and it only indirectly dealt with the political affiliations of the Apartheid Committee members.

A more radical move might have proven easier to get through parliament or the Financial and Foreign Policy Committees than the vague allegations about how funds were possibly misused. To convince the small centre parties in parliament was crucial for the acceptance of Guldberg's appropriation application. Several liberation movements produced texts and made speeches with a pro-communist rhetoric that Guldberg could have used as documentation, and unlike the Social Democrats the centre parties did not have personal relations with Neto, Tambo or others that could counter a claim that the movements were communist.

It is possible that Guldberg, when considering the Apartheid Appropriation set-up and its allocation practice in March and April 1974, had understood that K. B. Andersen's politically well advertised 1971/72 expansion in reality had meant only minor changes. Andersen had explained these facts in detail in Parliament, but this had been largely ignored by his critics, including Guldberg. They had focused on the international interpretation—the one that had been acknowledged by African presidents and which had upset the regimes in Pretoria, Salisbury and Lisbon—that liberation movements were to be directly supported. Andersen's critics could not, or would not, distinguish between the international 'political profiling' and the actual 'substance and practice' of the move. Consequently, there was not much for Guldberg to reverse when he succeeded Andersen. To revise the 1972 expansion would have been an important manifestation to Ove Guldberg and Venstre, and a general political blow to Andersen's Africa policies. But the criticism backfired and Guldberg had to find a different focus.

Concerning the Apartheid Committee, Ove Guldberg's initiative would not have dismantled it, but bypassed it politically and financially. The Committee would have been restricted to making recommendations for allocations within the UN system and, by and large, to only support Southern Africans in exile. On the other hand, it would still have been an influential reference on how the funds should be advocated among the various activities within the UN framework, including a continuous support to the liberation movements. As a matter of fact, several of the UN institutions that Guldberg attempted to boost support to supported liberation movements in exile. On the other hand, Guldberg's proposal could have served as a political platform for the Apartheid Committee to find and specify liberation movement activities and to earmark funding for them, through the UN organizations.[1]

---

1. Although the UN could not fund activities against the acceptance of a territory's government, the UN Trust Fund gave money to IDAF, mainly for legal assistance in South Africa. See Reddy 1999. Out of a total of DKK 10.2 million, the declined Guldberg appropriation application of 30 July 1974, which was turned down, included an allocation of 1.5 million to the UN Trust Fund of which most would have gone to IDAF.

Financially, the Danish NGOs and their international networks would have suffered by no longer being the main channels for Apartheid Appropriation funds. Some NGOs had many other activities, but to others, such as WUS Denmark, it would have been a serious blow. Ove Guldberg's initiative would have outmanoeuvred the NGOs in the Apartheid Committee and especially those with relations to the new left and student movements.

Stalemate

In his memoirs K. B. Andersen describes the day when Ove Guldberg's application was rejected as 'a beautiful day'.[1] To him, it probably was, because the line he had introduced in 1972 was being continued. However, the struggle with Guldberg and the narrow margin with which the Apartheid Appropriation supporters had won, also illustrates the limits for any further expansion. It explains why Denmark in 1974, and after, kept following a practice that basically had been established as early as in 1965/66, when the Apartheid Appropriation was started as a small humanitarian facility. Even if the allocations were increased from 1978, by between DKK 5 and 10 million per year, the practice was never changed, for instance along the lines of other Nordic countries that supported national liberation movements in cash, including for general running costs.

In February 1975 the liberal Venstre government resigned, after only 13 months in office. K. B. Andersen took over from Ove Guldberg as Minister of Foreign Affairs in a new minority Social Democratic government. Although Guldberg's initiative had not been approved, the political struggles over the political identity of the Apartheid Appropriation had fixed the front lines of Danish policy towards Southern Africa and the national liberation movements at a stalemate for the rest of the 1970s and well into the 1980s.

Andersen remained Minister until mid-1978 when he was appointed Speaker in Parliament. There were still skirmishes along this fixed front line concerning the Apartheid Appropriation and Danish Africa policy in general. For instance, Andersen was highly criticised when he received Frelimo's Marcelino dos Santos in April 1975 as a state representative (as a member of Mozambique's transitional government), when Denmark recognised Angola's MPLA government in February 1976 or when Andersen in November 1977, during a visit to Brazil, declared his recognition of Angola's right to request the assistance of foreign—Cuban—troops, just like West Germany had approved the presence on its territory of American, British and French troops after World War II.[2]

In his memoirs, K. B. Andersen quotes President Neto for thanking him when they met at Angola's Independence Anniversary in 1976. Neto was grateful for the continuity of Denmark's support and the positive attitude towards

---

1. Andersen, 1983.
2. KBAaba, Press cuttings, Vol I–VI (1975–1978).

MPLA despite changing Danish governments. 'I refrained from explaining how this continuity had been maintained', Andersen writes, referring to the struggle with Ove Guldberg.[1]

When it comes to making internationally noticed statements, Andersen's unspoken thoughts are right. But what Andersen misses is that he and Guldberg had a number of things in common. Like Andersen's own expansion of the Apartheid Appropriation in 1971–1972 had been of a political nature, Guldberg's initiative was also an attempt to change its political content rather than its 'substance and practice'. Guldberg's initiative would not have been the end to Danish support to MPLA and other liberation movements. Danish Africa policy could no longer have kept the same high political profile, but it would not have meant much for the financial continuity.

1. Andersen 1983, p. 33.

Chapter 5

Sanctions: Denmark's Shift from Hesitant to Decisive

In 1986, Denmark became the first Western country to impose full sanctions on South Africa, after maintaining for decades that such measures had first to be taken by South Africa's largest trading partners to have any effects. The process leading to sanctions began around 1978 and constitutes a second phase of Denmark's involvement in the struggle for liberation in Southern Africa. The interacting factors behind the process were the new international focus on events in South Africa after the Soweto uprising in 1976, increasing public and NGO pressure, a stronger UN commitment, plus, as the determining factor at the domestic political level, a change of attitude in the Danish Social Democratic Party.

Until 1978, the Danish debate focused on support through the Apartheid Appropriation, in particular support concerning national liberation movements. The debate reflects the dual nature of the Apartheid Appropriation, with the Ministry officials and NGO members on the Apartheid Committee running the administrative side, largely unruffled by the sometimes passionate political debates. The process leading to sanctions did not have this double dimension. It developed in the political realm only, without any interference from the administrative level. Danish sanctions were a result of the political debate that took place in parliament at a specific point in Danish political history, and of the continuous public pressure in the media and by the NGOs.

South Africa back on the agenda

For twenty years it was Nordic and Danish official policy that sanctions against South Africa were useless and even damaged the good cause if they did not include South Africa's major trading partners Great Britain, USA and France. This meant that the Nordic countries did not apply UN General Assembly resolutions that were made over the years, but awaited—and worked for—a mandatory decision from the Security Council. This had been Nordic policy since 1962, decided by the Nordic Ministers of Foreign Affairs, and it was followed by a majority of political parties in the Danish Parliament, including the Social

Democratic party. A minority of smaller socialist parties suggested changing this policy from time to time, but without success.[1]

Danish trade with South Africa was modest during the 1960s and the early half of the 1970s. Exports consisted mainly of machinery, and fluctuated with the signing of major individual contracts such as equipment to cement factories. Fruit was the main imported item, South Africa being the biggest supplier of foreign fruit in winter and spring.[2] But in 1976, Danish power companies started to buy South African coal. After the oil crisis in 1973, prices had gone up dramatically and parliament decided that Danish fuel imports should no longer be dominated by oil. Danish power companies went looking for suppliers, and at the same time South Africa was investing heavily in coal mining and exporting facilities. From a modest start of 21,000 tons in 1976, Danish purchases from South Africa increased to 384,000 tons in 1977 and 836,000 tons in 1978.[3]

This development coincided with South Africa once again becoming a political issue in Denmark. For ten years, only a few events in South Africa had reached the headlines in the international and Danish press. From a Danish perspective it seemed unlikely that apartheid would fall in any foreseeable future. As described in Chapters 3 and 4, the debates concerning Southern Africa concentrated mainly on what kind of support Denmark should provide, and to whom.

The Soweto uprising in 1976 changed this, and brought new dynamics into the situation in South Africa. Protesting students, the harsh reactions by the South African government and pictures of dead students upset the Danish public. People read in the newspapers about 'Bantu Education' and the dominance of Afrikaans in the schools. They witnessed the uprising, the strikes that followed, the growing unrest and the killing of Steve Biko in September 1977. South Africa was back on the agenda in Denmark, as it was worldwide, including in the UN. And suddenly there was a hope for change.

Nordic political response

In March 1977, the Nordic Ministers of Foreign Affairs were gathered in Reykjavik for one of their regular bi-annual meetings. Southern Africa was on top of the agenda, and the meeting adopted a number of guidelines to coordinate their policy. The Ministers stated that:

---

1. See Chapter 2 on how in the 1960s Danish and Nordic focus shifted from sanctions to humanitarian support. For the UN resolutions referred to in this chapter, see: United Nations, 1994. Between the end of the Rivonia trial in 1964 and Soweto in 1976 there were few proposals in parliament to take up sanctions, for instance after a large sale of Namibian 'Swakara' furs and after three Danish athletes' participation in the 'Pretoria Games', both in 1972. After Soweto, the number of motions and questions to Ministers etc. increased. Folketingets Forhandlinger 1972/72, F 3538 and F 4925, and Register of Foreign Policy readings in the Folketing, Vandkunsten 9/10.

2. Trade with South Africa was just 0.5 per cent of total Danish imports and exports (1973), Kirkernes Raceprogram, p. 35, 1974.

3. Hove et al. 1985, p. 198.

— the parties involved in the conflict in Zimbabwe should be brought to negotiating, and the illegitimate minority regime be replaced by majority rule, in order to secure a peaceful development;

— the South African occupation of Namibia was illegal. Free elections should be held under UN control and guidelines, and SWAPO involvement was considered crucial;

— the South African regime's oppression of the majority of its population was to be decounced. They encouraged solidarity with the African peoples struggle against the apartheid system. An arms embargo against South Africa was welcomed. The Nordic countries also expressed their wish for economic pressure against South Africa, and for the UN Security Council to take decisions aiming at preventing new foreign investments in South Africa.

— the information efforts of the Nordic volunteer organizations were acknowledged and fully supported.[1]

This joint reaction by the Nordic Ministers was a strong signal, but, once again, they did not challenge the steps already taken by the UN. It was merely a continuation of the Nordic strategy from 1962, of 'following the UN'. It was Danish policy that the Nordic governments continued this line. In the preparations for the meeting in Reykjavik, the Danish Ministry of Foreign Affairs summed up: 'Denmark has cut off relations with the minority regime in Salisbury and adheres strictly to the sanctions against Rhodesia from 1966. Denmark complies fully with the arms embargo against South Africa called for by the Security Council'.[2] The profile was high on Rhodesia, where the UN had adopted full sanctions after the Ian Smith regime had declared unilateral independence from Britain in 1965. On South Africa the meeting made a reference to what steps the Security Council was preparing.

At their next meeting, on September 1–2 in Helsinki, the Foreign Ministers discussed Southern Africa again. In their final statement, the Ministers again strongly condemned South Africa's apartheid regime, and invited the international community 'to take concrete action to show its solidarity with the struggle against the apartheid system'.[3] Compared to the previous statement, this appeal went one step further. The wording now included indirect pressure, also on the UN Security Council, to impose stronger measures. With respect to their *own* role in the international community, the steps of 'concrete action' were however cautious: the Ministers agreed to establish a Working Group to study options for a joint Action Programme concerning further economic measures against South Africa.[4]

In March 1978, the Foreign Ministers met again, this time in Oslo. On the basis of the findings of the Working Group established in Helsinki, the Nordic countries for the first time not only coordinated guidelines for the individual

---

1. Communique from meeting in Reykjavik, 23 March 1977. MFA 6.U.566.
2. Memorandum 11 March 1977. MFA 6.U.566.
3. Communique from meeting in Helsinki 1–2 September 1977, WUS 11.4.
4. In Denmark, the establishing of the Working Group was by some experienced as a result of Swedish hesitation as that country's stronger economic involvement would have stronger domestic economic and employment effects. Interview with Åkjær 24 September 1997. For contemporary documentation on Swedish business involvement, see Magnusson 1974.

countries to follow, but a joint 'Action Programme' on a 'foreign policy' issue. It was agreed:

— to prevent new Nordic investments in South Africa;
— to negotiate with Nordic companies to reduce their production in South Africa;
— to request sports and cultural contacts to be terminated;
— to increase support to refugees, liberation movements and victims of apartheid.
It was agreed that other measures should be added at a later stage.[1]

The Action Programme was not a call for state sanctions. The agreement covered some, but not all aspects of the relationship with South Africa. Trade was not mentioned, nor was legislation or other measures to enforce the programme. The Nordic official policy was a call for private action.

However, it was the first time the Nordic countries went beyond UN obligations, and it manifested to South Africa that there were countries in the West prepared to embark on economic measures. The Danish press described the Action Programme as 'going further than previous international sanctions'. 'Stop Nordic New Investment in Vorster's South Africa', one headline said. 'The programme is a considerable tightening of policies against South Africa while at the same time being realistic', newspapers reported. But they also commented that the important thing was what concrete measures were taken as a follow up of the Action Plan.[2]

The relatively soft content of the Action Programme shows that the Nordic countries were still influenced by a concern for what was realistic policy, as they had been since 1962. Sanctions would not influence Pretoria if imposed by the Nordic countries alone, and they would harm Nordic industry and business at a time of economic hardship in the Nordic countries. In Sweden, a commission was established during 1978, to look at what kind of initiatives would not damage the Swedish economy too seriously.

Coordinating with the EC

In the first half of 1978 Denmark chaired the European Community (EC). At the conference of Foreign Ministers in Copenhagen, February 1978, British Foreign Secretary, David Owen, told Danish newspapers that 'anyone who thinks the EC should work for sanctions is a fool'.[3] This was only a few months after the Danish Minister of Foreign Affairs, K. B. Andersen, had argued in an interview that the EC would lose credibility if it did not follow up on its verbal criticism of South Africa, formulated at its previous summit in July 1977.[4]

K. B. Andersen chaired the Foreign Ministers' conference, and tried to combine his visions for a stronger EC commitment with considerations of what

1. Communique from Meeting of Nordic Foreign Ministers. Oslo 9–10, March 1978. EE.
2. *Politiken* and *Aktuelt,* 11 March 1978.
3. *Ekstra Bladet, Politiken.* 15 February 1977
4. *Information,* 26 November 1977.

could realistically be adopted. In a comment, he reduced the implications of Owen's statement to a technical discrepancy on what specific measures should be taken: 'Everybody can agree to declare himself against South Africa's policy', he stated.[1] To K. B. Andersen, the challenge was to find the balance between formulations that all countries could agree on, but had no consequences, or such that would have binding implications and—therefore—could not be adopted. Attempts to make the EC agree on any kind of action would have implications on Denmark's room for manoeuvre both unilaterally and in the Nordic forum. Similarly, as preparation for its EC presidency, Denmark had voted cautiously during the 1977 UN General Assembly compared to previous years. This was criticised by the left wing opposition parties but must be seen as an attempt to make space for reaching an EC agreement.[2]

Danish concerns the Foreign Ministers' conference proved right: The resolutions that could be adopted at the EC summit in June 1978 were limited. The EC agreed to criticise South Africa for its apartheid racism and for its occupation of Namibia, and confirmed previous proclamations that the regime should be opposed through economic measures. But no specific interventions could be agreed upon. It was only agreed to start administrative preparations of possible sanctions. This procedure was rather similar to the Nordic process started the year before, when the Nordic Ministers had established their working group Action Programme.[3]

Danish policy on the Nordic Action Programme

In November 1977, the Socialist People's Party (SF) had proposed a motion in the Danish Parliament, referring to the UN General Assembly sanctions programme of November 9, 1976, and to the increasing Danish coal purchases in South Africa. It was forwarded to the Foreign Policy Committee and the readings coincided with the Nordic meeting of Foreign Ministers in March 1978. The SF motion was modified and served as the basis for the Danish action plan on the Nordic Action Programme that was adopted in its final form on 26 May 1978. The Danish Parliament:

— declared its support for the Action Programme,
— invited the government to work out specific initiatives in accordance with the pro
  gramme,
— requested the government to terminate export credits for South Africa and phase out
  the Export Officer based at the Pretoria embassy, and
— requested Danish power companies to stop their coal purchases in South Africa.[4]

---

1. Ibid.
2. MP Steen Folke of Venstresocialisterne summed up Denmark's voting in the UN in 1977 compared to other years and other countries in a feature in Politiken 2 May 1978.
3. *Politiken, Ekstra Bladet,* 13 June 1978.
4. Folketingets Forhandlinger 1977/78: A1625, F4892, C637. Bramsen 1990, p. 234. Hove et al. 1985, p. 240.

The original SF proposals to stop Scandinavian Airline Systems (SAS) from flying on South Africa and to stop migration to South Africa did not find sufficient backing by the ruling Social Democratic Party, and were not included.
The motion did not imply any formal legislation, and as such it followed the
traditional pattern of the Nordic attitude on the matter since 1962. The Nordic
countries had likewise abstained from voting in favour of the 1976 UN General
Assembly sanctions programme that SF had used as a reference for its proposal. It was considered too comprehensive, and Denmark once again chose to
follow the decisions made by the Security Council.[1]

This pattern was to remain in place for a few more years, until political constellations changed and it had been proved that requests and invitations to private business did not influence coal purchases and other economic relations
with South Africa. It also reflects the limited influence the UN General Assembly resolutions in general had on its member states: as long as sanctions were
not mandatory, nations and individual businesses did not consider moral issues
superior to financial matters. The result was a very limited impact on South
Africa's apartheid politics.

No restrictions on the coal trade

Before its first purchase of South African coal in 1976, the semi-official
regional Danish power company ELSAM had asked the Danish Ministry of
Trade for comments and they were told that there were no restrictions. The
first imports were a success, and there was political pressure in Denmark to
rely more on coal than on oil. Also, the quality of the South African coal was
good, and the prices were low even though the oil crises of the 1970s had created a sellers' market. Later, after Soweto, ELSAM explained that there had
been no signals or requests from the Danish government not to buy its coal in
South Africa. 'If we were asked to, the trade would stop immediately' the
chairman of the board stated to the press.[2]

In June 1978 the Ministry of Foreign Affairs wrote to the companies doing
business with South Africa. To ELSAM the central formulation was: 'The government would welcome it if ELSAM could reach the conclusion that it would
serve ELSAM's own interests to purchase coal from other producers than South
Africa'. However, ELSAM chose to prioritise its business interests. The chairman of the board commented: 'We have received the letter, but will take no further action. The request is not a prohibition'.[3] A few days later, ELSAM signed
a large contract to buy more coal from South Africa.

ELKRAFT, the other major Danish power company, followed and also
bought South African coal. By the end of the 1970s, the two companies to-

---

1. During the debate on the SF motion, Foreign Minister K. B. Andersen refused to use the General
   Assembly Sanctions Programme of 9 November 1976 as an argument for Danish action, because
   Denmark had not voted for it. Folketingets Forhandlinger 1977/78, F4892.
2. *Politiken*, 29 September 1977.
3. *Socialistisk Dagblad*, 2 August 1978.

gether imported about 30 per cent of the fuel for Danish electricity supplies from South Africa, about 10 per cent of the total Danish energy consumption. This was to remain the case until 1983–84. Seen from a South African perspective, Denmark represented about 10 per cent of South Africa's coal exports.[1]

ELSAM's reaction reflects the lack of effect the requests from the UN, Nordic Ministers and the Danish Parliament had on companies and individuals to voluntarily phase out their economic and other contacts with South Africa.

Revenue and bottom line figures had the upper hand: from 1978 to 1984 Danish exports to South Africa grew from DKK 150 to 700 million and imports from DKK 224 to 1,263 million (of which coal amounted to DKK 1,129 million), in current prices.[2]

Public action

After 1976, the increasing number of reported human rights violations in South Africa, combined with statistics showing that trade relations were expanding despite expressed political concern, was a paradox that mobilised individuals and organizations in Denmark. From 1977, local South Africa Committees were established in several towns by local branches of the socialist SF and VS parties, local committees of the Danish NGO 'Mellemfolkeligt Samvirke' (MS), and by people with links to 'Kirkernes Raceprogram' (KR), the Danish branch of WCC's 'Programme to Combat Racism'. They demonstrated against shops selling South African fruit and agitated for stronger government measures against South Africa, for boycotts and sanctions. The movement started at the same time as SF proposed its motion in parliament and as the UN discussed South Africa and decided on an arms boycott, a few months after the news of the death of Steve Biko in September 1977.[3]

The campaign resulted in the large supermarket chain 'Irma' and the cooperative 'Brugsen' dropping South African products, and in consumer commodity imports going down. Brugsen's decision was the result of KR members being elected to the boards of local Brugsen shops. After many of the individual shops decided on a boycott, a national boycott was proposed at the central level, and got a majority backing.[4] Irma, a private chain, reluctantly made its decision by the end of 1977. It openly declared that protesters' campaigning outside its shops damaged business and that it had no other alternative than to sanction South African products.[5]

Danish NGOs, together with labour and other organizations, as well as the bigger South Africa Committees (SAKs) in Copenhagen and Århus, organized a major conference on March 17–18, 1978, with the participation of Danish Ministers and Members of Parliament, ANC and SWAPO representatives and

---

1. *Politiken,* 29 September 1977. Buksti, 1979. Hove et al. 1985, p. 198–203.
2. Hove et al. 1985, p. 160. Built on figures from the National Danish Statistical Bureau.
3. Binders 2 and 46. LSA/SAKK.
4. Interview with Max Kruse 14 January 1997.
5. *Børsen,* 14 May 1979.

Danish and international organizations. This was less than a week after the Oslo meeting of the Nordic Ministers of Foreign Affairs, and at the beginning of the UN Anti-Apartheid Year that started a few days later, in memory of the Sharpeville-massacre on March 21, 1960. Danish Social Democratic Prime Minister Anker Jørgensen opened the conference, and ANC President Oliver Tambo and SWAPO Representative Hadino Hishongwa described the situation in South Africa and Namibia. They asked for assistance to the liberation movements and for a full boycott of South Africa, although they still did not ask directly for government sanctions. Abdul Minty, from the British Anti-Apartheid Movement, presented a ten-point programme that he invited Denmark to follow. It called for a stop in private investments, a stop in the increasing coal purchases, a stop in government export subsidies, visa regulations, sports boycott and stopping flights by the Scandinavian airline SAS. But he did not call for comprehensive trade sanctions or for an official Danish ban on trade.[1]

In March 1978, the 'Landskommiteen Sydafrika Aktion' (LSA) was established to coordinate NGOs, South Africa Committees, trade unions, party branches and individuals during a national campaign inspired by the UN Anti-Apartheid Year 1978. The campaign worked with information, lobbying and fund raising, often in connection with demonstrations outside shops selling South African fruit and other products.

The chairman of LSA, Max Kruse, was one of the founders of Kirkernes Raceprogram, but soon it seemed to many of its individual members and member organizations that LSA was to a large extent run and funded by people and trade unions connected to the Communist party.[2] Social Democratic organizations withdrew from LSA, and Mellemfolkeligt Samvirke introduced conditions for their continued membership. They demanded transparency in the organization, as well as a veto against LSA initiatives for strikes and picketing.

In 1979, LSA continued to campaign actively, in particular through information on the conditions in Southern Africa and a continuous agitation for sanctions. Funds were raised and donated to ANC for equipment for its 'Radio Freedom' in Lusaka, and a printing press for the exiled trade union SACTU's newspaper 'Workers Unity'. Local committees in several Danish towns gave the movement quite a wide national backing, and spectacular actions were carried out to attract press attention and spread information.

As in the 1960s, the issue of apartheid's constitutional racism and the violations of human rights were able to mobilise a considerable part of the Danish public. And people wanted the government to impose official sanctions to isolate South Africa. The public demanded measures that went well beyond the

1. *Information,* 18–19 and 20 March 1978, *Aktuelt,* 18 and 20 March 1978. Among organization representatives were also SACTU President Drake Lekota, E.S. Reddy from UN Center against Apartheid, South African writer Ruth First and Craig Williamson from IUEF.
2. 'LSA was clearly dominated by communists, very nice and loyal people whom I have much respect for and who could really work hard.' Interview with Max Kruse, 14 January 1997. *MS-Avisen,* January 1979. Interview with former LSA Secretary Janne Felumb 31 October 1997.

diplomatic requests made by the anti-apartheid representatives from Southern Africa.

Coalition Government 1978–1979: Cease-fire on sanctions and support

During 1978, the political constellations in Denmark changed fundamentally. Minister of Foreign Affairs, K. B. Andersen, resigned in July to become the Parliament Speaker. On August 30, the 'SV-government', a coalition between the Social Democratic party and the liberal Venstre, was formed.

When in opposition, Venstre had strongly criticised K. B. Andersen for the way he handled the expansion of the Apartheid Appropriation in 1971–72. In turn, the Social Democratic Party had fought Venstre's Minister of Foreign Affairs, Ove Guldberg's initiative to roll back the expansion during the 1974 Venstre government. On the question of boycott opinions also differed. For instance when the Danish Parliament adopted the May 26 1978 motion that Danish policy should follow the Nordic Action Programme on trade and investment measures, the Social Democratic Party had voted for and Venstre against.

The new coalition demanded a compromise, and Southern Africa ceased to exist as a field for political debate. There was a stalemate along the frontline of Denmark's support to the liberation movements, and gradually the struggle died out. Ove Guldberg had left parliament in 1977 and Poul Hartling had become UN High Commissioner for Refugees in 1978. Minister of Foreign Affairs in the new government was Henning Christophersen, the new Chairman of Venstre. During the coalition government, Venstre did not bring up either the Apartheid Appropriation or the Apartheid Committee. Sanctions were not discussed. Christophersen's appropriation applications to the Finance Committee all followed the recommendations of the Apartheid Committee.

The coalition government marked the end of a period starting in 1971, when the Apartheid Appropriation had been high on the Danish political agenda. With the independence of Angola and Mozambique in 1975, the controversial support to their liberation movements ended. Soweto had put South Africa back in the spotlight, but the Danish debate now centred on sanctions rather than on devloping the Apartheid Appropriation humanitarian support to Southern African liberation movements. Initially, South African movements and organizations did not have the same kind of direct contacts with Danish NGOs and politicians as those of the Portuguese colonies. Such support did not develop until the mid 1980s when NGOs promoted it in the form of educational support to refugee camps in Tanzania.

After 1978, Denmark's official support through the Apartheid Appropriation was regularly increased without any significant discussions. From 1974/75 to 1978 the Apartheid Appropriation had only increased from DKK 12.5 to 14.9 million. In 1978 the appropriation only covered nine months, as the financial year was changed to follow the calendar year. And in 1979, the appropriation was raised to DKK 25 million, with reference to the UN anti-apartheid year and to Danish support lagging behind that of Sweden and Norway. In 1980 it was raised to DKK 35 million, and from 1981, it was routinely increased by DKK 5 million per year.

On the other hand, the SV-government was not in a position to make any moves concerning sanctions. In October 1978, when it was learned that ELSAM had signed new contracts and intended to increase its coal purchases, the left socialist party Venstresocialisterne (VS) put forward a motion in Parliament based on the 10-point programme that Abdul Minty had promoted at the conference in March. They proposed that the government should prohibit investments in South Africa, stop coal purchases immediately, stop sports and other cultural contacts and within six months end all Danish trade with the country. Henning Christophersen, the new Minister of Foreign Affairs, could not accept the motion, repeating the motivation from the previous 15 years that unilateral Danish sanctions would have no effect. The Spokesman of the Social Democratic Party stated that further Danish steps would have to be taken in an international context.

One step towards international coordinated action came in September 1978, at the General Debate in the UN, when Henning Christophersen argued that the arms embargo was hardly sufficient to convince the regime in South Africa to change its apartheid policy. During a debate in the Danish parliament, VS pointed to the unlikely prospect of the USA and Great Britain voting for mandatory measures in the Security Council, and to the fact that Denmark would not at all stand alone if it did impose sanctions: It would be following India and other countries in Asia and the Middle East. The statements show the political positions in Denmark. The social democratic, liberal and conservative parties still followed the pattern of not anticipating effectively coordinated international action, whereas the socialist parties and the social liberal party (Radikale Venstre) wished to do so.[1]

The SV-government was dissolved in October 1979, and a new minority Social Democratic government took over, without changing the Danish policy on sanctions. The new government retained the Nordic 1962 position. In the following years, the left wing opposition forwarded motions and posed questions to the Ministers 14 times. These initiatives were often coordinated with NGO activities, and often the political parties got background information provided by NGOs and their international contacts, such as the British and Dutch Anti-Apartheid Movements and the 'Shipping Research Bureau' in Amsterdam.

The opposition insisted that the government should follow up on the Nordic Action Plan and legislate against coal purchases, oil transports, and investments and tighter visa regulations, but with no tangible results. In his answer

---

1. *Politiken,* 27 October 1978. Foreign Minister Christophersen's speech in the UN 26 September 1978, SD.upol.aba. Folketingets Forhandlinger 1978/79. S 1038.

to the last in the series of questions before the next change of government in 1982, Minister of Foreign Affairs Kjeld Olesen explained that 'Danish efforts would have to be based on the Nordic Action Programme adopted by the Danish parliament 26 May 1978, meaning that the Nordic countries should work for proposals in the UN Security Council leading to mandatory boycotts of trade with South Africa. Another element in the Nordic Programme is requesting that sports and cultural contacts cease'.[1]

Increasing attention on increasing trade

Danish trade with South Africa had not been significant until it became totally dominated by the coal imports, as described above. After the modest start in 1976, imports were grew to a rather constant 3 million tons from 1979/80, about 10 per cent of South Africa's coal exports worth more than DKK 1 billion. Other Danish trade with South Africa which inceased was shipping.[2]

From the end of 1979 to the beginning of 1981, Danish shipping lines, especially Maersk Lines, were involved in oil transports to South Africa. After the Islamic Revolution in Iran and a visit there by ANC, the oil exports to South Africa from Iran and OPEC member countries in general were stopped. Oil became a major concern for South Africa, as three quarters of its imports had been delivered by Iran. A complicated alternative network of suppliers and transporters was established, and it often worked in secrecy. Maersk was involved in these transports and is estimated to have transported 20–25 per cent of South Africa's oil imports in the years around 1980. As described above, among the fruitless motions discussed in the Danish parliament in the same period, it was suggested, in March 1981, to prohibit oil transports and oil exports to South Africa by law. The motion was not passed.[3] Despite this, Maersk noticed the changing winds and withdrew from its involvement. The company only participated in one more transport, in 1983.

Danish NGOs and especially the South Africa Committees (SAKs) focused the public eye on the increasing trade relations. The contradiction between the clear statements of the Nordic Ministers of Foreign Affairs, and the meagre results of the softened Danish May 26 1978 motion seemed an obvious paradox to many Danes. It strengthened the NGO notion that legislation on sanctions was necessary.

The typical activity of local SAKs was a combination of public demonstrations, information and lobbying efforts. Actions against shops selling South African commodities, wholesale fruit markets, offices of importers/exporters trading with South Africa, or against coal terminals, provided a basis for handing out material and informing the press. The information material was often

---

1. Reply of 13 August 1982 to question (no 1085, Folketingets Forhandlinger 1981/82) of 6 August. EE.
2. Hove et al., p. 198, based on *Financial Times* and Danish Bureau of Statistics.
3. Folketingets Forhandlinger 1980–81, B98. Hove et al., p. 228–229. Hengeveld and Rodenburg (eds) p. 21, 165–168.

based on careful research into statistics on trade, company registers etc., supplemented by international research from the Anti-Apartheid movement in
Britain and others. Research findings were also distributed to politicians. In
September 1979, Bishop Desmond Tutu, General Secretary of the South African Council of Churches visited Denmark as the guest of DanChurchAid. At a
press conference on TV he repeatedly defined the increasing Danish coal purchases as 'disgraceful'. The statement was also noted by parts of the Danish
public that normally considered sanctions as too radical a step, and upon his
return to South Africa, Bishop Tutu had his passport withdrawn.[1]

A new Government—another new majority

In 1982, the Social Democratic minority government resigned and a conservative-liberal government took over. This was another minority government,
based on the support of the centrist, social liberal party 'Radikale Venstre'
(RV). RV agreed with the government that solving Denmark's economic and
financial problems was to have top priority. However, on a number of international and defence issues, RV and the new government disagreed. South Africa
was one of them, as it had been during the previous government.

Simultaneously, the Social Democratic Party, now in opposition, was developing its position on official sanctions. No longer in government the party was
not hampered by the need to balance political measures towards South Africa
with considerations for the fragile Danish economy and unstable political alliances.

To the Social Democrats the Southern Africa question and other international issues also presented an opportunity to bring down the new government.
In Denmark, it was parliamentary tradition that a government resigned when it
faced a majority opposition in parliament on foreign policy and other central
issues. The new conservative-liberal government however soon demonstrated,
during numerous debates and motions, that it was able to bypass this tradition
by simply abstaining from calling a vote when faced with defeat, or living with
the defeat. Because its domestic policy had the necessary backing, the government knew it would not be met with a vote of no confidence, which would otherwise be expected in such situations. The price to be paid was that the
government had to accept that parts of Denmark's foreign policy were directed
by the opposition, in such cases dubbed 'the alternative majority'. This is what
opened the way for Danish official sanctions.[2]

The first example of a parliamentary decision by 'the alternative majority' is
from January 1983. During a debate in Parliament, the Social Democratic

---

1. Tutu 1984, p. 18. Interview with Kruse, 14 January 1997.
2. In particular missile deployment and disarmament issues in Europe became the subject of heated
   discussions, and the new Venstre Minister of Foreign Affairs, Uffe Ellemann-Jensen, would often
   have to travel to NATO meetings and other international fora with a mandate he disagreed with,
   but nevertheless chose to live with.

Party moved a resolution that got the expected backing from the government support party RV, and the two socialist parties, SF and VS. The resolution stated that the government should set a time limit and request Danish power companies to phase out their coal purchases in South Africa before 1990.[1] The government spoke against it during the debate, but abstained from voting, in order not to be defeated on the issue. Not surprisingly the government evoked the position of previous Social Democratic governments, and their argument that further sanctions would have to be part of a coordinated UN effort based on mandatory Security Council resolutions. Otherwise they would only damage the Danish economy. But the Social Democratic Party explained that its patience had now finally run out because of the continuing coal purchases. The government survived, the resolution was passed and a new parliamentarian pattern was set for the coming years.

The following year, visa regulations, illegal arms transport by a Danish ship and oil transports by Danish shipping lines were debated in the Danish parliament. Despite Denmark's declared policy against apartheid there were still no visa restrictions for South Africans coming to Denmark. The Danish press revealed that Danish ships had been involved in smuggling arms to South Africa since 1978, despite the ban that Denmark had adopted in connection with the UN arms embargo of 1977. The Danish Seamen's Union collected reports and documentation from its members on shipping activities, including photos of a Danish coaster entering Durban harbour flying the yellow flag signalling a cargo of explosives and of tankers transferring oil cargoes at sea to disguise their origin. The Minister of Trade and Industry was asked in parliament to stop oil transports according to the Nordic Action Programme, but the government was not prepared to take any action. They claimed that the only result would be to do damage to the competitiveness of Danish shipping.[2]

In February 1984, the Socialist People's Party (SF) party moved a new resolution. As a follow up to the January 1983 resolution and the Nordic Action Programme of 1978, the wording was relatively soft compared to the party's position during the debates, but the purpose was to gain support from the Radikale Venstre and the Social Democratic Party.

The resolution demanded that:

— Danish power companies should report their coal purchases and what initiatives they were taking to follow the 1978 and 1983 requests to gradually end their purchases from South Africa before 1990;
— the government should make it clear to shipping and oil companies that trading oil with South Africa was contradictory to Danish legislation;
— the Danish government should work actively against Nordic involvement in IMF credits to South Africa;

---

1. Folketingets Forhandlinger 1982–83. F 4511.
2. Hengeveld and Rodenburg (eds) 1995 p. 92, 297. Folketingets Forhandlinger 1982–83: F 7460, 8252, 11283, 13290. 1983–84: F 1514.

— the government should, if necessary through legislation, prevent any new Danish investments in South Africa;
— flight connections to South Africa by the Nordic airline SAS should cease immediately.

The resolution was referred to the Standing Foreign Committee, which debated it at length. After being modified, it was passed on May 29, with the omission of the SAS issue and the request that coal purchases should be gradually terminated. The Committee was aware that most other European airlines had flights to South Africa, with connections to Copenhagen as well as to Sweden and Norway, and that Norway and Sweden were not prepared to stop the flights of their jointly owned Nordic SAS airline. The Foreign Policy Committee also noted that a ban on Danish tankers would merely lead to tankers from some other country taking over.[1]

The government was against the resolution during the first reading, in the Foreign Committee and during the second and final reading when it was passed. They repeated the argument that sanctions would have to be international and mandatory. Like the 1983 motion, the SF resolution still used the word 'requests' when talking about coal purchases and oil supplies. But it was qualitatively new that these requests had a built-in time factor and that parliament had committed itself to passing legislation if the companies did not follow the requests. Regarding investments, the government argued that there was no legal basis for the motion, but in response, 'the alternative majority' asked the government to produce such a basis if necessary. The resolution was passed on the 29th, against the vote of the government.

The following year the government respected the resolution, although it did not approve of it, and in February 1985 it proposed a bill against new investments in South Africa. It was modified to include Namibia too, and to instruct Danish companies already involved in South Africa to report regularly on their activities, wage rates and other conditions for their employees. The bill was passed in May with the government parties abstaining from the vote.[2]

Political steps towards Danish sanctions

In the early 1980s, around and after the change of government in Denmark in 1982, South Africa experienced a build-up of domestic protests against the regime and its violent oppression. In August 1983, the United Democratic Front was formed as a protest against plans for a new three-cameral constitution in the country, excluding black influence, which was adopted the following year. Demonstrations, boycotts of local elections and a wave of other protests, where hundreds were killed, made the regime declare a state of emergency in July 1985. Thousands were arrested, but this neither reduced the protests nor the killings. In August, President P.W. Botha declared that the South African

---

1. Folketingets Forhandlinger 1983–84. B 7, F 1638, F 7137. Sanctions on oil transports had been requested by the UN General Assembly in 1975, without effect.
2. Folketingets Forhandlinger 1984–85 L 194.

regime 'had crossed the Rubicon' and would never give up racism as its foundation. Internationally, this was seen as Pretoria's decisive manifestation of not being prepared to compromise. A Danish editorial analysed the situation as follows: 'Pressure from abroad and the threat of black demonstrations spreading, have pushed the development ahead... Botha's policy will not lead to a democratic South Africa.'[1]

In September 1984, the Danish daily 'Politiken' and the Swedish 'Dagens Nyheter' gave their 'Freedom Prize' to Winnie Mandela and Helen Suzman at a combined conference and ceremony in Copenhagen. Mandela's daughter, Zenani Dhlamini, received the prize on behalf of her mother. The main speaker was rector of Copenhagen University, Ove Nathan, who underlined the need for solidarity with the struggle against apartheid and referred to European Nazism in the 1930s and 40s as well as modern racism. Among the panellists were former newspaper editors Per Wästberg and Donald Woods, ANC Representatives Marius Schoon, Florence Maleka and Lindiwe Mabuza, all of whom recommended trade and other sanctions against South Africa.[2]

Danish NGOs and South Africa Committees (SAKs) continued their lobbying and actions. Around 1980, the umbrella network 'National Committee for South Africa Action' (LSA) had lost backing from member organizations frustrated with the influence of the Communist Party. In 1981 it was financially paralysed after an unexpectedly expensive tour by the 'Amandla' performance group in November 1980.

Instead, especially the 'Kirkernes Raceprogram' (KR) and the local SAK in Århus continued to dig up documentation on the trade between Denmark and South Africa. Other NGOs were also increasingly active in information and lobby work, based on their contacts and project activities in the Southern Africa region, many funded by the Apartheid Appropriation. In 1981, Mellemfolkeligt Samvirke established the coordinating body 'Fællesmøderne' ('The Joint Meetings') to help NGOs exchange information and plans and to coordinate contacts with the politicians.[3]

The NGOs analysed the coal trade, and documented how the low South African prices were the result of 'apartheid discounts' to maintain a market, as more and more customers phased out their purchases. Thus, as SAK-Århus pointed out, the argument that Denmark should go for the cheapest coal on the world market, without making any political considerations was in itself a political free-ride on other countries' sanctions. In 1985 KR published a comprehensive profile of Danish trade, investments and other economic involvements in South Africa, a follow up to their pioneer book from 1974.[4]

1. *Politiken,* 17 August 1985.
2. *Politiken,* 1 October 1984.
3. Interview with Janne Felumb, 31 October 1997. Talk with Morten Nielsen, 9 April 1996. Talk with Claus Bornemann, June 1996.
4. Letter to the editor by Erik Tang of SAK Århus. *Politiken,* 6 June 1985. KR's book 'Byggeklodser til Apartheid': Hove et al. 1985.

From 1982, SAK-Århus ran a boycott campaign against South African coal by lobbying the local town council, and during 1985, Århus and other major Danish towns voted to boycott South African products, referring to the various resolutions in parliament and to UN Security Council Resolution no 569 of July 26, 1985. These resolutions were in fact moved by Denmark and France and invited UN member states to take various measures against South Africa. There was some discussion if local government bodies were allowed to get involved in foreign policy, but the initiatives soon got quite a wide local political backing. The point made was that the municipalities, in their function as individual economic bodies, had to comply with the same parliamentary and government requests that private companies, shipping lines and power companies were expected to follow. The individual municipality suffered few negative consequences by omitting South African products from their shopping lists. A more important side effect was that the local government representatives on the semi-official Danish power company boards were instructed to pressure the managements to speed up the phasing out of their South African coal purchases.[1]

In 1984–85, LSA was re-established as a loose umbrella structure for local SAKs, and a new active SAK-Copenhagen was established. In the years to come, it carried out a lot of spectacular activities to inform about the situation and human rights violations in South Africa, and it was a strong advocate for Danish sanctions legislation. The actions in Copenhagen were not always legal, but always based on the self-defined moral foundation that representatives of a system that did not provide equal rights to its citizens should not expect to enjoy such rights themselves. In May 1985, South African Airlines and a Danish trading company had their office furniture, typewriters etc. 'forcibly removed' into the streets 'in solidarity with the three million blacks who had been deported', as LSA put it.[2]

On August 28, 1985, it was reported that a United Democratic Front protest march to the Pollsmoore prison in Cape Town, where Nelson Mandela was held, had been interrupted by the police leaving several killed, and that UDF leader Allan Boesak had been arrested the day before. The Copenhagen SAK demonstrated in the city streets, acting out the Pollsmoore march as a performance.[3]

In October 1985, the South African consulate in Copenhagen was occupied. A major police force managed to clear the premises before a press conference could be held, but the occupants got hold of the consulate's codebook, which was hurried to ANC in Lusaka. 8 activists were sentenced to 60 days of

1. *Information*, 4, 5, 6 August 1985. Politiken 10 September.
2. *Politiken*, 3 May, Information 24 May 1985
3. *Politiken*, 30 August 1985.

Danish activists acted out the Pollsmore march in the centre of Copenhagen, 20 October 1985.
(Photo: Polfoto)

The 'South Africa Committee, Copenhagen' occupies the South African consulate in Copenhagen,
30 October 1985, as a protest against South African police arrests at the Pollsmore march. In the morning
the Danish police stormed the consulate and arrested the occupants, but only after files and code books
had been removed and taken to the ANC. (Photo: Gert Jensen/Polfoto)

mitigated imprisonment. Charges were raised to have them pay for the damage, but the lawsuits that could have ruined them individually, were never followed up by the Danish legal system.[1]

In November 1985, SAK in Copenhagen invited toy manufacturer LEGO to stop its exports to South Africa. LEGO refused. The unions of kindergarten teachers and assistants immediately launched a boycott calling on kindergarten staff to stop purchasing LEGO. Before Christmas, demonstrations were carried out in shopping centres, in the Copenhagen town hall square etc, to discourage parents from giving LEGO as Christmas presents to their children.[2]

The Nordic path

As the conflict in South Africa intensified in 1985, the international attention increased even more. In March 1985, the Nordic Ministers of Foreign Affairs met in Helsinki and discussed updating the Nordic Action Programme of 1978. The initiative came from Norway that had experienced a strong public debate about South Africa in connection with Archbishop Desmond Tutu receiving the Nobel Peace Price in December 1984. The other countries backed the proposal, and Sweden and Denmark referred to their plans for legislation against investments in South Africa.

The Norwegian proposal was to work for more coordinated international initiatives and to have the Nordic countries carry out a list of measures in the mean time. These included a stop in investments, and of the SAS flight connections and effective measures to stop private trading and financial connections between Nordic companies and South Africa. The plan was slightly modified by the Nordic Working Group of officials that had been established in connection with the Nordic 1978 Action Programme, and adopted at the Ministers' next meeting in Oslo on October 17–18. The revised Action Plan was not radical. It basically implemented UN Security Council resolutions to ban arms trade, military computers or Kruger-rand gold coins and nuclear cooperation, stopped Nordic credits to South Africa and banned Nordic investments in South Africa, as Sweden and Denmark had already decided. The plan requested private businesses to reduce their trade with South Africa or local production in the country, and finally, it implemented Nordic restrictions on visa regulations and sports, as well as cultural and scientific contacts. The most important impact of the plan was the political effect of all the Nordic countries agreeing on the measures and declaring their wish for effective and mandatory sanctions.[3]

---

1. *Ekstra Bladet*, 30 October, *Politiken*, 31 October 1985. Talk with Morten Nielsen, 9 April 1996.
2. *Information*, 4 December 1985. 'Børn og Unge' no 47, 5 December 1985.
3. Replies 8 May 1985 by Minister of Foreign Affairs to the Parliamentary Foreign Affairs Committee, EE. Ministry of Foreign Affairs internal note 2 August 1985 on draft Nordic Action Programme of 24 July, MFA 6.U.566. Communique from meeting of Nordic Ministers of Foreign Affairs 17–18 October 1985, MFA 6.U.566. *Information*, 19 October 1985.

Within the Danish trade union movement there was a growing demand for action, in particular from the skilled workers union (SiD). In September 1985 dockworkers considered a boycott against South African coal imports to Danish power companies. In October, SiD announced a boycott on all transport of South African products, in collaboration with transport workers in Norway and Sweden.[1]

It became an issue for the entire Danish Trade Union Congress (Landsorganisationen, LO), and from November 18, 1985, a two and a half month trade union boycott of South Africa was launched[2]. The immediate effect was that a shipment of coal, arriving a week later on a Dutch ship for a power station in the town of Åbenrå, was refused permission to unload under much media attention.Later, another two ships arrived at Åbenrå and could not be handled. The boycott was taken to the Court of Arbitration where the employers claimed that according to existing rules, apartheid could not form the basis for a boycott. There was no ongoing trade conflict in South Africa that Danish workers could claim solidarity with, and the goals of the boycott went beyond labour issues. LO claimed that such a strict interpretation of the labour agreements would prevent any action when it was most needed, and that trade union activities were suppressed by the South African regime.[3]

Completing Danish sanctions

After the May 1985 bill on Danish business involvement in South Africa, the opposition parties in the Danish parliament kept asking the government for further action on the Danish coal purchases.[4] On the second day of the new 1985–86 parliamentary session in October, the Social Democratic Party moved a resolution to impose another round of economic sanctions. These were quite comprehensive: An embargo on oil trade and transport, measures to quickly end coal purchases, stop for all other imports by June 1, 1986, and financial support to ANC and SWAPO, including an ANC representation office in Copenhagen. In November, the government proposed an alternative motion that did not specifically ban trade, but included yet another invitation to companies to voluntarily cease their involvements and trade with South Africa.

The motions were debated in parliament and in the Foreign Policy Committee. The Social Democratic proposal was supported, due to the alternative opposition majority, but the formulations were softened in order to reach a compromise with the government parties. The proposed economic sanctions were boiled down to requesting the government to legislate a six months phasing-out of coal imports and an immediate stop to all other trade.

1. *Politiken,* 10 September 1985.
2. *Information,* 18 October 1985.
3. *Information,* 26 November and 7 December 1985.
4. Questions to the Minister of Foreign Affairs from the standing Foreign Policy Committee 30 August 1985. Reply from Minister 23 September, EE. Questions in Parliament 4 and 18 September 1985, Folketingets Forhandlinger 1984-85, S 11960 and 12088.

Support to ANC and SWAPO was not mentioned, as the Committee found that Denmark already supported them through the Apartheid Appropriation and that the government was strongly against any additional support. Also, the Social Liberal Party (Radikale Venstre), that joined the opposition majority on foreign policy issues but otherwise supported the government, was hesitant about supporting ANC. On December 13, 1985 the revised Social Democratic motion was approved in Parliament. The Prime Minister and the Minister of Foreign Affairs had been quite positive during the process, but in the end, four of the government parties abstained from voting, as one of the minor government parties (Centrum-Demokraterne) was against any kind of sanctions.[1]

By December 22, the trade unions had called off the transport boycott, before the Court of Arbitration could announce whether or not the boycott was a violation of labour regulations. Even if the unions had a good case on the moral level, their position was weak in relation to the actual text. The trade union leaders knew this, and they now announced that the government was about to impose sanctions through legislation, and that the goals for the boycott had been reached.[2]

As in 1985, the government 'behaved' and produced the legislation required in the December 13 resolution. On January 30, 1986, it proposed the 'Bill against coal imports from the Republic of South Africa'. It was adopted after the normal readings on May 6 with the votes of the opposition as well as the government. The bill prohibited coal imports after a six-month period, three years before the deadline requested by Parliament in 1983.[3]

On March 21, the government presented the 'Bill against trade with the Republic of South Africa', covering all other imports and exports. Its first reading on April 15 exposed the continued discrepancy between the government and the opposition majority.

The Minister of Foreign Affairs, Uffe Elleman-Jensen, opened his speech by declaring that he proposed the bill without pleasure, and he did not welcome the backing he knew it would get. In the debate, the government parties regretted that Denmark alone should impose general trade sanctions on South Africa and move ahead of the other Nordic countries, Denmark's EC partners and the UN Security Council resolutions. Economically, they said this was playing into the hands of Denmark's competitors, and that the Danish economy, employment and balance of payment would be severely damaged. South Africa, on the other hand, would barely notice the efforts. The government further referred to the Swedish position when the Nordic Action Programme was revised in Octo-

---

1. Motion B1, Folketingets Forhandlinger 1985–86. Debate 27 November 1985, Folketingets Forhandlinger 1985–86, F 2918. Reply 9 December 1985 from Minister of Foreign Affairs to the Foreign Affairs Committee on Danish and other support to ANC and SWAPO. EE. Report from Foreign Policy Committee 10 December on Motion B1. EE. Interview with SF spokesman Søren Riishhøj, Land og Folk 12 February 1985. Motion 13 December 1985, Folketingets Forhandlinger 1985–86, F4674.
2. *Information*, 17 and 19 December 1985.
3. Folketingets Forhandlinger 1985–86, L 160.

ber 1985, recommending that the Nordic countries should not legislate on general sanctions. Similarly, Denmark should continue to appeal to companies to cease their engagements in South Africa voluntarily. The Minister ridiculed the opposition parties for being out of touch with reality (the Socialist People's Party) and out of touch with responsibility (the Social Democratic Party), for not caring about the loss of business, work places and opportunities to gain foreign currency.[1]

The opposition majority in their turn described Elleman-Jensen as being the one out of touch with reality, expecting to convince Great Britain and the United States to impose sanctions in the near future. They saw no other options than getting as many countries and groups of countries as possible to move ahead and try to motivate others. The opposition recognised that sanctions would not be without costs for Denmark, but found them to be very modest compared to the sufferings of the black population in South Africa. They were also confident that the other Nordic countries would soon follow Denmark's example, and—teasing the Minister—they said they trusted him to use his diplomatic skills to bring his Nordic colleagues in line with Denmark.[2]

After being referred to the standing Foreign Policy Committee, the opposition majority parties strengthened the bill by omitting from the sanctions a clause that excluded a number of commodities that government found crucial for Danish industry. Instead they opened up for a two-year period of grace after the application of the bill. Services were included along with commodities, and oil transports on Danish vessels were explicitly mentioned. The bill in its new form was passed on May 30, 1986. The government abstained from voting. As from December 15, trade with South Africa was banned, marking the final step away from the Nordic 1962 policy of 'following the UN'.[3]

A peculiar parliamentary situation

The political developments in South Africa in the 1980s can be described as the push factor for the Danish sanctions: the increasing volume of information about human rights violations in South Africa motivated the Danish population and created a pressure on the Danish political system. The public challenged the government and the political parties to take action. But sanctions were not introduced after Soweto or the killing of Steve Biko in 1976–77 when there were plenty of reasons for doing so, and when Danish coal purchases increased dramatically. Events, news reports and global public attention constituted a continuous push factor, but still the official Danish position remained unchanged from 1962 until 1982. The situation in South Africa landed on the doorstep of the Danish political system as a result of increasing global atten-

---

1. Folketingets Forhandlinger 1985–86 F 9727.
2. Ibid.
3. Reports from Foreign Policy Committee 15 May and 22 May 1986 on Bill L 228. Folketingets Forhandlinger.

tion, but it was taken or 'pulled' inside only through a change of government creating a peculiar parliamentary situation.

In late 1980, Social Democratic Minister of Foreign Affairs Kjeld Olesen said in Parliament: 'As long as the UN Security Council has not adopted sanctions against South Africa, it is unrealistic that the Nordic countries do it. The government opposes isolated Danish initiatives, but is willing to work within the UN to increase international pressure against the white South African minority regime'.[1] This was a comment on the socialist parties' and the Social Liberal Party' attempt to move a resolution on a coal purchase ban and general sanctions.

The same parties later formed 'the opposition majority' together with the Social Democratic Party, but not until the change of government in 1982.[2]

No longer in government, the Social Democratic Party adopted the left wing opposition's views on sanctions. In terms of mandates, this led to the opposition now constituting a majority in parliament, able to force the government to work for a policy it was actually against. The opposition controlled the official Danish policy on sanctions, as well as some other foreign policy issues—notably security and disarmament in Europe. This did not lead to a vote of no confidence to bring the government down, because one of the members of the 'majority opposition', the Social Liberal Party (Radikale Venstre) supported its strict economic and fiscal policy. They did not want a change of government. This unique parliamentary constellation gave room for the opposition resolutions that propelled the change in the Danish sanctions policy and brought it ahead of UN requests and mandatory measures, and even ahead of fellow Nordic countries.[3]

In this sense, Minister of Foreign Affairs Uffe Elleman-Jensen had a point when he criticised the Social Democratic Party for being 'out of touch with responsibility' when they supported sanctions in 1986. The shift in the party's position would not had happen if it had not been a part of the opposition, and it was yet to happen in the other Nordic Social Democratic Parties. But the Social Democrats and the rest of the opposition majority also had a point when predicting that the other Nordic countries would follow Denmark, and that the Danish move would become something much more than a futile demonstration only damaging the Danish economy. In September/October 1986 the United States Congress adopted comprehensive sanctions against the will of ruling President Ronald Reagan as the second country in the Western world, in a process somewhat similar to the one in Denmark.

1. Folketingets Forhandlinger 1980–81: Resolutions B20 and B 35.
2. Folketingets Forhandlinger F 1983. *Information*, 13 November 1980.
3. Interview with Jørgen Estrup, 11 July 1997. Kelm-Hansen,1992.

Chapter 6

Trends and Conclusions

This study has focused on significant shifts in Denmark's official support to Southern Africa during the era of colonialism and apartheid. These shifts reveal what players were around and what factors ultimately proved decisive for the development of Danish policy. A number of conclusions can be drawn from the study. First, it shows that the Danish approach can be divided into two main periods; the first concentrating on financial support to victims of apartheid (1960–78) and the second on financial and political sanctions (1978–1992). Second, different actors developed and formed Danish policies in these periods, namely politicians, state officials, NGOs and other representatives of Danish civil society. And they played different roles in the two mentioned periods. Third, the official Danish support and its political impact was of a flexible nature. The technical/administrative substance of the support on the one hand, and the political profile on the other, were not always linked, and their development was to a large extent formed by domestic issues.

Main periods

1960–78 official Danish policy towards southern Africa was to develop and provide *financial support* to the struggle against racism and imperialism in Southern Africa. This policy was inspired by public attention and the involvement of NGOs, trade unions, youth organisations, political parties in their capacity as grass roots structures and of committees established to express solidarity and lobby official policies. The impetus in the first half of the 1960s was the brutality of the South African regime, as shown in the Sharpeville massacre, the banning of ANC and PAC and the trials against the political leaders of these organisations. The news from South Africa gave the Danish public insight into the racist apartheid system, and most parts of the Danish society denounced it. This mobilisation was not exceptional for Denmark; apart from the other Nordic countries it also took place in Britain, Holland, USA and many other Western countries.

However, only in the Nordic countries did popular mobilisation develop into official political measures, in the form of systematic official financial support to victims of apartheid. In Denmark, official humanitarian support was launched in 1964/65 when the Apartheid Appropriation was established. This humanitarian tool to assist victims of apartheid soon came to include the whole Southern African region.

In 1971/72, the support was expanded to also benefit the civil activities of liberation movements, and at the political level it was to give the support the maximum international political effect. In 1974, a minority government tried to limit the influence of Danish NGOs on official policy making, but had to give this up. At these three points in time Danish official support policies were debated in public, political arguments were aired and many administrative considerations were made.

In the second important period, from 1978–92, *sanctions* are the core issue. The Soweto protests, the death of Steve Biko and the widespread popular protests in South Africa in the 1980s revived the focus on the country, after a period of relative indifference. A peculiar domestic political situation led Denmark to apply official trade sanctions after decades of maintaining that such measures were fruitless and would even damage the cause.

Actors

Two major groups of actors/participants constituted the 'Denmark' that sought to contribute to national liberation in Southern Africa: official institutions representing the state, and private and popular NGOs.

In brief, the official institutions and the state:

— criticised the Southern African regimes bi-laterally and in international fora for their colonialist and racist policies;
— financially supported victims of the regimes through international and Danish NGOs. Support was granted to projects/activities run by:
  a) National Liberation Movements (NLMs), and
  b) Humanitarian and human rights organizations (including church organisations) (e.g. IDAF, WCC, IUEF);
— used the financial support actively as a basis for political pressure on the regimes in Southern Africa;
— imposed unilateral financial and trade sanctions on Rhodesia and South Africa but not on NATO/EFTA partner Portugal.

Danish NGOs:

— supported NLMs, and NGOs in Southern Africa with their own limited funds;
— carried out information, documentation and lobby activities, to raise public awareness of the situation in Southern Africa and to develop and expand the official support;
— channelled and helped administer official support;
— made and developed direct contacts with organisations and NLMs working in Southern Africa.

However, this study also shows that alternative classifications are also possible. In significant periods, the parties involved have to be grouped differently.

From 1960 to 1978, two sets of players were involved in developing and providing *financial support*. One set consisted mainly of politicians and the press, and these players formed the debate and brought forward the arguments. Another set were the officials in the Ministry of Foreign Affairs together with the involved group of NGOs in the Apartheid Committee who cooperated in hammering out the actual support. These sets of players are surprising compared to the more traditional roles of the state institutions and NGOs listed above. They are also surprising in the light of how little connection there was between them in some of the major shifts in Danish policies.

We have seen that the political and public debate was remarkably independent of how the support was administered and the funds actually allocated. In the 1970s the debates were rather fierce, in the press as well as in parliament. Meanwhile, the actual implementation practice was carried out and gradually developed at the administrative level, by the Apartheid Committee. These two sides of Danish support could be called the 'political profiling' and the 'substance and practice' of the Apartheid Appropriation.

This dual landscape can be seen as the result of the procedures established for the Apartheid Appropriation and the Apartheid Committee in 1964/65. Until then, things were more 'traditional' with NGOs acting as part of the public sphere, lobbying and campaigning, and the official administration functioning as a vehicle for the political and parliamentary system. It is interesting to note that the establishing of the Apartheid Appropriation was the result of a not so unusual process where public debate influenced political decision and government initiatives.

Through the Apartheid Committee, Danish NGOs came to play a unique role cooperating with the government and in particular with the administration. Instead of influencing policy from the outside, they became an integrated—though sometimes inspirational—part of how the Apartheid Appropriation was administered. They followed its gradual development closely, under the authority of the Ministry of Foreign Affairs, and usually did not participate in the public debate about it.

It is also significant that when the support was expanded in 1972, it was a 'new' organisation (the re-organised World University Service Denmark (WUS) with a new structure and new people) with highly public activities that became the channel for the first expanded support. Later, WUS-Denmark was subsequently integrated in the Apartheid Committee structures and procedures. As a consequence, the NGOs were not a factor that renewed Danish support between 1964/65 and 1978, when the focus turned to official sanctions.

The period from 1978 was different. *Sanctions* were debated among politicians, both in the media and in parliament, supplemented with contributions and arguments from news editors and others. In contrast to the *support period*, the same politicians now developed actual policies. The elements were hammered out at the political level; there was not a parallel body with a high level of detailed knowledge and authority to form Danish sanction policies as there had been with support. Parliament formed Denmark's sanctions. The major role of the NGOs in this period was their traditional one; to lobby, campaign and seek to focus the public debate. NGOs were still represented on the Apartheid Committee and participated in allocating the official Apartheid Appropriation funds. New partnerships were established to act as channels for new activities, and the funding volume was gradually increased. But no new initiatives came from the Apartheid Committee as regards policy developments, the nature of support or the character of channelling organisations.

Double nature and flexibility

In both periods, Danish involvement in the struggle against racism and colonialism in Southern Africa was simultaneously of a humanitarian and a political nature. The balance between these two aspects fluctuated over time, and the specific form of the Danish support, through the Apartheid Committee arrangement and the involvement of the NGOs, made it very flexible.

Some Danish initiatives were of a strict *political* nature. They were sometimes covered in the international press, also in Southern Africa and Portugal where the regimes reacted to the political pressure. A constant minimum official pressure was expressed in the UN and other international fora. This pressure consisted of official denunciations of racism and colonialism and encouraged the regimes in Pretoria, Salisbury and Lisbon to reform. Domestically, NGO manifestations constituted the public critique of the regimes, e.g. through inviting prominent representatives from liberation movements to visit Denmark. These kinds of pressure resemble what happened in other Western countries, and did not affect the regimes in Southern Africa. One example is the Nordic initiative in 1964 to make the UN contribute to reform in South Africa. The attempt received wide international backing, but proved fruitless because South Africa refused to cooperate at all. Until the Soweto uprising triggered a new momentum for UN initiatives in 1976, the UN was left with minimal influence on South Africa.

Denmark's *humanitarian* support consisted of financial assistance to organisations actively opposing the regimes or working to reduce the effects of oppression. This came to include civil activities of the national liberation movements. Education, health, legal assistance and food aid were the main fields of support to Southern Africa—including to liberated areas—and to refugees in exile. The support was of a genuine humanitarian kind, and motivated partly by the notion that victims of racism and colonialism should not be denied development assistance similar to what many of the new states in Africa received. From this point of view the humanitarian support enjoyed a wide backing in Denmark.

However, supporting humanitarian organisations and the civil activities of liberation movements in Southern Africa also had obvious political dimensions:

— It represented an acknowledgement of the need and moral righteousness of counteracting the regimes. Thereby, it signalled that Denmark took sides in the conflicts, denounced the regimes, acknowledged the liberation movements and invited other Western countries to side with them too.
— The humanitarian support also indirectly provided the liberation movements with more resources for their political and military struggle. This dimension was the most controversial and did, for instance, trigger considerations (and sometimes fierce debates) about whether or not Denmark was violating international law or, in a cold war bi-polar scenario, possibly supporting communist enemies.

How Danish support developed into having both a humanitarian 'substance and practice' side and a 'political profile' side, has to do with the actors involved, as described above. In substance and practice Danish support developed as a humanitarian facility. This was obvious during the first years of the Apartheid Committee/Apartheid Appropriation arrangement, and it was still the case when, in 1971, the first humanitarian support was given through a national liberation movement. Nobody outside the Apartheid Committee, not even the sitting right-liberal government, noticed or saw this as a shift away from humanitarian practice. But from then on, the liberation movements' share of the allocations gradually increased.

This development was relatively unaffected by and independent of the high political profile Minister of Foreign Affairs K. B. Andersen attributed to the appropriation both internationally and nationally. This dominated the political debates in the early and mid 1970s. But even if Andersen made loud political exclamations about the changed objectives of the Apartheid Appropriation, it did not mean that the 'substance and practice' was actually any different from before.

On the other hand, the debate about the 'political profile' of Denmark's support took place with only limited reference to the actual 'substance and practice'. The political profile must be seen as an independent and rather spectacular aspect of Danish support, developed in Parliament, in the press and in the public debate.

The double nature of Danish humanitarian support meant that it could be construed in two ways:

1. as humanitarian aid to refugees and victims of racist or colonial oppression; or
2. as assistance to and sanctioning of certain movements involved in military struggle against independent states.

This is what made Danish official support politically flexible: Denmark could insist that its support was strictly humanitarian, as was done in its early years, for instance when Southern African regimes protested that Danish support was against international law, or in some of the domestic debates. At the same time, from the 1970s, Denmark could rightly maintain that it supported national liberation movements with substantial funding. This was emphasised for instance during K. B. Andersen's visits to Africa and when Denmark participated in the increased international criticism of the regimes.

References

Unpublished material

Archives

EE   Eric Erichsen (private collection).

FKNra   Archive of 'Folkekirkens Nødhjælp' (DanchurchAid) in 'Rigsarkivet' (The Danish National Archives), Copenhagen.

FKNår   'Folkekirkens Nødhjælp årbøger' (DanchurchAid annals). Unpublished annual collection of minutes, reports, clippings etc, in DanChurchAid, Copenhagen.

KBAaba   K. B. Andersen's archive in 'Arbejderbevægelsens Bibliotek og Arkiv' (The Labour Movement Library and Archive), Copenhagen.

KBAra   K. B. Andersen's archive in 'Rigsarkivet' (The Danish National Archives), Copenhagen.

KG   Kirsten Gauffriau (private collection, now in 'Rigsarkivet')

KR   Archive of 'Kirkernes Raceprogram' (Danish Programme to Combat Racism). At: Ecumenical Centre, Århus.

LSA/   Archive of the 'Landskommiteen SydafrikaAktion' (National Committee–South Africa

SAKK   Action) and 'Sydafrika Komiteen København' (Copenhagen South Africa Committee)

LV   Leif Vestergaard (private collection)

MFA   Ministry of Foreign Affairs, files:
          5.Q.45a: 'Communism in Africa'
          5.Q.293: 'African Liberation Movements'
          6.U.566: 'Humanitarian and Educational Assistance to Suppressed Groups and Peoples'
          6.U.566/1,2,3 etc: Ibid., with special reference to individual receiving organisations.

MS   Archive of 'Mellemfolkeligt Samvirke', in 'Rigsarkivet' (The Danish National Archives), Copenhagen.

SAK-Å   Archive of 'Sydafrika Komiteen Århus' (Århus South Africa Committee)

SD.upol.   Social Democratic Party's Foreign Policy Committee, in 'Arbejderbevægelsens Bibliotek

aba   og Arkiv' (The Labour Movement Library and Archive), Copenhagen.

WUS   World University Service–Denmark's archive. Today: 'Ibis', Copenhagen.

Interviews

Ben Amathila, 20 November 1996, SWAPO Chief Rep to the Nordic Countries and Germany.

Ole Bang, 12 May 1997, General Secretary Danish Refugee Council 1960–65, Vice Chairman Danish 'Council for South Africa', Vice President IDAF 1966–68, Member of the 'Apartheid Committee' 1966–93.

Niels Bentzen, 16 April 1996, WUS activist 1977, Project Officer 1978, Member of the 'Apartheid Committee' 1976–89 for DSF and WUS.

Arne Piel Christensen, 14 May 1997, General Secretary Danish Refugee Council 1967–1997. Member of the 'Apartheid Committee' 1967–93.

Steen Christensen, 9 January 1997, Member of the board for Workers Solidarity Fund 1969–93; International Secretary of the Social Democratic Party 1980–84 and General Secretary 1984–97; Member of the 'Apartheid Committee' 1979–93.

Jørgen Estrup, 11 July 1997, MP Radikale Venstre (Social Liberal Party) 1984–2000.

Janne Felumb, 31 October 1997, Coordinator LSA (National Committee on South Africa action) 1978–1981.

Bent Honoré, 3 May 1997, MP for Kristeligt Folkeparti 1973–79.

Max Kruse, 14 January 1997, Activist in Kirkernes Raceprogram 1971-78. Chairman LSA 1978–79. Project Officer in DanchurchAid 1978–85. Member of DCA board 1985–97, Chairman from 1990. Member of the 'Apartheid Committee' for DSF 1972–75.

Lindiwe Mabuza, 15 July 1997, ANC Chief Representative to the Nordic countries.

Viggo Mollerup, 3 January 1997, DCA 1964–76, General Secretary from 1966. Member of the 'Apartheid Committee' 1966–75.

Carsten Nørgaard, 7 November 1996, Project Officer in WUS 1981–90. WUS Coordinator for Namibia 1990–96.

Kjeld Olesen, 21 August 1997, MP Socialdemokratiet 1966–79. Minister of Foreign Affairs 1979–82.

Peder Sidelmann, 3 December 1996, Activist in Afrika-71 and WUS 1969–72, WUS Project Officer 1972–76. Member of the 'Apartheid Committee' for WUS 1971–76.

Kjeld Åkjær, 24 September 1997, International Secretary LO (TUC) 1972–93. Member of the 'Apartheid Committee' 1974–89.

Talks

Christian Balslev-Olesen, February 1986, Activist in Kirkernes Raceprogram 1972–78. Project Officer in DanChurchaid 1985–88, Regional Representative in Southern Africa 1988–90, General Secretary from 1990.

Claus Bornemann, June 1996, MS General Secretary, 1978–89, Member of the 'Apartheid Committee' 1991–92.

Peter la Cour, 18 August 1997, Chairman of the Conservative Students' organisation.

Erich Erichsen, 18 April 1996, MS Information Officer 1973–88.

Steen Folke, 18 March 1996, MP, Venstresocialisterne

John Hansen, April 1997, South African refugee, working in ANC office Denmark.

Patricia Hansen, June 1996, Activist in 'Anti-Apartheid Denmark' 1976–88.

Kirsten Gauffriau, 18 March 1997, Activist in Namibia Committee and Namibia Campaign, 1974–1981

Flemming Gjedde-Nielsen,14 March 1996, WUS activist, member of board 1981–86. Epesus House 1985–86. WUS Programme Officer from 1987.

Gorm Gunnarsen, April 1997, Central SAKK/LSA Activist from 1984, Chairman.

Erik Jørgensen, May 1997, Activist in PCR 1984–97, Chairman from 1995.

Poul Jørgensen, 10 June 1997, UFF/DAPP Spokesman. Member of the Apartheid Committee 1987–91.

Christian Kelm-Hansen, 23 May 1996, DUF General Secretary 1955–59, Chairman 1959–62. Danish Red Cross General Secretary 1959–65. MS General Secretary 1965–69. Board for Development Assistance 1962–89, Chairman from 1975. MP SocDem 1979–90.

Henning Kjeldgaard, August 1997, International Secretary, Danish Social Democratic Youth 1959–60. Danish Ambassador in Dar-es-Salaam and Harare 1983–93.

Claus Larsen-Jensen, September 1996, SiD (Skilled Workers Union) International Secretary 1982–1998.

Barry Levinrad, 2 August 1996, South African refugee 1980–90, working with SACTU-Nordic office, Copenhagen.

Erik Lyby, June 1996, Activist in SAK-Århus starting 1978. Active in the MS South Africa group, member of MS board 1979–83.

Morten Nielsen, 9 April 1996, LSA/SAKK Central Activist 1982–93

Peter Schoubye, 27 May 1997, Member of Conservative Students' Organisation

Ejnar Søndergaard, February 1997, Activist in SAK-Århus and MS. LSA chairman.

Leif Vestergaard, April 1996, PCR Coordinator 1971–72, Member of DCA Board 1974–95.

Klaus Wulff, 17 September 1996, Afrika-71 and WUS Activist and Programme Officer 1970–78. Member of Apartheid Committee for DSF and WUS.

Published material

Books

Adler, Elizabeth, 1974, *A small Beginning: An assessment of the first five years of the Programme to Combat Racism.* Geneva: World Council of Churches.

Andersen, K.B, 1983, *I alle de riger og lande.* Copenhagen: Gyldendal.

Befrielseskampen i Namibia, 1980. Ulfborg: Tøj til Afrika.

Bislev, Sven, Henrik Jensen and Viggo Plum, 1971, *Den Økonomiske og Politiske Udvikling i Det Sydlige og Østlige Afrika.* Copenhagen: Afrika-71.

Bramsen, Christopher Bo, 1990: *Sydafrika, Kamp eller Dialog.* Copenhagen: DUPI.

Brix, Carl Otto, 1994, "Partisoldaten der blev forladt af kompagni A", *Vandkunsten 9/10, 205.*

Buksti, Søren, 1979: *Danmarks forbindelser med Sydafrika.* Copenhagen: Landskomiteen Sydafrika Aktion.

Christensen, Steen, 1971, *Befrielsesbevægelserne i det sydlige Afrika,* Copenhagen: SOC.

Christensen, Steen and Alex Frank Larsen (eds), *Det lænkede Afrika: 20 kritiske artikler om det tiltagende opgørt med Venstres politiske og økonomiske dominans.* Copenhage: SOC.

Collins, John: Southern Africa: Freedom and Peace: Addresses to the United Nations 1965–1979. (Collected for the internet at: www.anc.org.za/ancdocs/history/solidarity)

Eriksen, Tore Linné (ed.), 2000, *Norway and National Liberation in Southern Africa.* Uppsala: Nordiska Afrikainstitutet.

Gunnarsen, Gorm, 1995, *Sydafrikas Historie.* Copenhagen: Gyldendal.

Hengeveld, Richard and Jaap Rodenburg (eds), 1995, *Embargo: Apartheid's Oil Secrets Revealed.* Amsterdam: Amsterdam University Press.

Hove, Ole, Jørgen Iversen and Jesper Jørgensen, 1985, *Byggeklodser til Apartheid: Dokumentation af Danmarks økonomiske forbindelser med Sydafrika.* Århus: Kirkernes Raceprogram. (Parts of the book were published in English in 1987, *Bricks to apartheid: Denmark's economic links South Africa.* Århus: Kirkernes Raceprogram.)

Hækkerup, Per, 1965, *Dansk Udenrigspolitik.* Copenhagen: Fremad/AOF.

Kelm-Hansen, Christian, 1981, "Brydningstid—herhjemme og ude i verden", in: Arskov, Niels Peter (ed), *At politisere ungdommen—Dansk Ungdoms Fællesråd 1940–1980.* Copenhagen: DUF.

Kelm-Hansen, Christian, 1992, "Dansk Sydafrikapolitik". Speech held at South Africa Conference 5 February 1992. Printed in *Orientering fra Kirkernes Raceprogram 3,92.*

Kirkernes Raceprogram, 1974, *Danmarks aktier i Apartheid & Co.* Århus: Kirkernes Raceprogram.

Knudsen, Poul Erik, 1989, "Kirkernes Raceprogram i Danmark—en udfordring til kirken", In: Nørgaard-Højen (ed.), 1989.

Knudsen, Poul Erik and Erik Jørgensen (eds), 1988, *En evangelikal kommentar til krisen i Sydafrika og Kairos-dokumentet.* Århus: Det Økumeniske Fællesråd.

Krag, J.O. and K. B. Andersen, 1971, *Kamp og Fornyelse: Socialdemokratiets Indsats i Dansk Politik 1955-71.* Copenhagen: Fremad.

Legum, Colin and John Drysdale, 1970, *Africa Contemporary Record: Annual Survey and Documents 1969–70.* Exeter: Africa Research Limited.

Lodberg, Peter, 1988, *Apartheid og de Lutherske kirke.* Århus: Anis.

Magnusson, Åke, 1974, *Sverige—Sydafrika : en studie av en ekonomisk relation.* Uppsala: Nordiska Afrikainstitutet. (An English abstract was published as: *Swedish investments in South Africa.* Uppsala: Nordiska Afrikainstitutet. 1974.)

Marks, Shula, 1999, "Half-Ally, Half-Untouchable". Paper presented at the conference *The Anti-Apartheid Movement: A 40-Year Perspective.* London.

Minty, Abul, 1963, *Sandheden om Sydafrika*. Copenhagen: Danmarks Socialdemokratiske Ungdom.

Nørgaard-Højen, Peder (ed), 1989, *På Enhdens Vej*. Copenhagen: Anis.

Reddy, E.S, 1986, *Nordic Contribution to the Struggle against Apartheid: Its Evolution and Significance*. (An edited version of a presentation made at the Nordic Africa Institute, Uppsala, 11 February 1986. Published on the internet at: www.anc.org.za/ancdocs/history/solidarity/uppsala.)

Reddy, E.S, 1999, Defence and Aid Fund and the United Nations: Some Reminiscences, Draft paper submitted to University of Witwatersrand. (Published on the internet at: http://www.anc.org.za/un/reddy/index.html#COLLECTIONS)

Schori, Pierre, 1994, *The Impossible Neutrality—Southern Africa: Sweden's Role under Olof Palme*. Cape Town: David Phillip.

Sellström, Tor, 1999(a), *Sweden and National Liberation in Southern Africa*. Uppsala: Nordiska Afrikainstitutet.

Sellström, Tor, 1999(b), *Liberation in Southern Africa. Regional and Swedish Voices*. Uppsala: Nordiska Afrikainstitutet.

Skovmand, Sven, 1969, *FN, Sydafrika og menneskerettighederne*. Copenhagen: Dansk Samråd for Forenede Nationer.

Socialdemokratiet, 1969, *Det Nye Samfund—70'ernes politik: Socialdemokratiets arbejdsprogram, vedtaget på den 30. Kongres, juni 1969*. Copenhagen: Fremad.

Soiri, Iina and Pekka Peltola, 1999, *Finland and National Liberation in Southern Africa*. Uppsala: Nordiska Afrikainstitutet.

Sydafrikakomiteen i København and Afrikagrupperna i Sverige, *UDF—fællesfront mod apartheid*. Copenhagen: Sydafrikakomiteen i København.

Tang, Erik, Arne Wangel and Peter Weigelt, 1981, *Namibia undertrykkelse og frihedskamp*. Copenhagen: Mellemfolkeligt Samvirke.

Tutu, Desmond, 1984, *Skabt i Guds billede*. Copenhagen: Folkekirkens Nødhjælp, Det Økumeniske Fællesråd, Kirkernes Raceprogram.

Tøj til Afrika, 1980, *Befrielseskampen i Namibia*. Ulfborg: Tøj til Afrika

United Nations, 1994, *The United Nations and Apartheid 1948–94*, New York: Department of Public Information.

United Nations Centre against Apartheid, 1978, 'Tribute to Canon Collins', *Notes and Documents, 22/78*. New York: United Nations Centre against Apartheid. (Also published on the internet at: http://www.anc.org.za/ancdocs/history/solidarity/collinsp.html).

Wittrup, Steen Stub, 1982, *Sort Hverdag* Århus: Aros.

Wangel, Arne, 1985, *Namibia—Et folks eksistens står på spil* Copenhagen: WUS.

Periodicals

Newspapers:

Aktuelt	Social Democratic daily
B.T.	Independent daily
Berlingske Tidende	Conservative daily
Børsen	Business daily
Ekstra Bladet	Independent daily
Frederiksborg Amtsavis	Liberal regional daily
Information	Independent daily
Jyllandsposten	Right-liberal daily
Kristeligt Dagblad	Christian daily
Land og Folk	Communist daily
Næstved Tidende	Liberal regional daily
Politiken	Social Liberal daily
Socialistisk Dagblad	Daily affiliated to the 'Venstresocialisterne' party
Vestkysten	Liberal daily

Others:

Børn og Unge	Monthly magazine of kindergarten staff trade union 'BUPL'.
Den Ny Verden	Third World Research quarterly. Copenhagen: Oversøisk Institut/Institut for Udviklingsforskning/Center for Udviklingsforskning (Centre for Development Research)
Folketingets Forhandlinger	(Parliament proceedings) in Folketingstidende. Published by Schultz Grafisk, Copenhagen.
Finansudvalgets Aktstykker	(appropriation applications to parliament's standing Financial Committee) published by Schultz Grafisk, Copenhagen.
Lederbladet,	Dansk Ungdoms Fællesråd.
Løn og Virke	Trade Union Magazine. Landsorganisationen De Samvirkende Fagforbund (Danish TUC).
MS-Avisen	Monthly Bbulletin of the NGO 'Mellemfolkeligt Samvirke'.
Politisk Revy	Independent socialist monthly magazine on politics and social issues. 1963–87
Trade Union Information Bulletin	Landsorganisationen De Samvirkende Fagforbund. (Danish TUC)
Vandkunsten	Periodical on conflict, politics and history. Copenhagen: Eirene.

Appendix

Danish Governments 1960–1993

	Prime Minister	Minister of Foreign Affairs	Party/parties
1960	Viggo Kampmann	Jens Otto Krag	S, RV
1962	Jens Otto Krag	Per Hækkerup	S, RV
1964	Jens Otto Krag	Hækkerup/Hans Tabor	S
1968	Hilmar Baunsgaard	Poul Hartling	RV, V, K
1971	Jens Otto Krag	K. B. Andersen	S
1972	Anker Jørgensen	K. B. Andersen	S
1973	Poul Hartling	Ove Guldberg	V
1975	Anker Jørgensen	K. B. Andersen/A Jørgensen	S
1978	Anker Jørgensen	Henning Christoffersen	S, V
1979	Anker Jørgensen	Kjeld Olesen	S
1981	Anker Jørgensen	Kjeld Olesen	S
1982	Poul Schlüter	Uffe Ellemann-Jensen	K, V, KrF, CD
1987	Poul Schlüter	Uffe Ellemann-Jensen	K, V, KrF, CD
1988	Poul Schlüter	Uffe Ellemann-Jensen	K, V, RV
1990	Poul Schlüter	Uffe Ellemann-Jensen	K, V
1993	Poul Nyrup Rasmussen	Niels Helveg Petersen	S, RV, CD, KrF

S	Social Democratic Party
RV	Social Liberal Party (Det Radikale Venstre)
V	Liberal Party (Venstre)
K	Conservative Party (Det Konservative Folkeparti)
KrF	Christian Democrats (Kristeligt Folkeparti)
CD	Center Democrats (Centrum-Demokraterne)

Table 1. Danish official support from the Apartheid Appropriation via LO (Danish TUC) (DKK)

	South Africa	Zimbabwe	Namibia	Angola	Mozambique	Total
1964/65						
1965/66						
1966/67						
1967/68						
1968/69						
1969/70						
1970/71						
1971/72						
1972/73						
1973/74						
1974/75						
1975/76	150,000					150,000
1976/77	320,000	150,000	50,000			520,000
1977/78	500,000	70,000	140,000			710,000
1978	875,000		200,000			1,075,000
1979	617,500	372,500				990,000
1980	1,280,000	1,705,000				2,985,000
1981	2,500,000					2,500,000
1982	3,000,000					3,000,000
1983	4,400,000					4,400,000
1984	5,600,000					5,600,000
1985	4,550,000					4,550,000
1986	5,309,000					5,309,000
1987	7,062,000					7,062,000
1988	7,830,000					7,830,000
1989	10,592,500					10,592,500
1990	12,983,403					12,983,403
1991	12,055,062					12,055,062
1992	13,222,757					13,222,757
1993	7,445,000					7,445,000
Total	100,292,222	2,297,500	390,000			100,292,222

Table 2. Danish official support from the Apartheid Appropriation via DanChurchAid—WCC/LWF (DKK

	South Africa	Zimbabwe	Namibia	Angola	Mozambique	Total
1964/65						
1965/66						
1966/67	45,000					45,000
1967/68	42,000					42,000
1968/69	82,000	25,000				107,000
1969/70	36,500	18,250			18,250	73,000
1970/71	93,750	46,875			46,875	187,500
1971/72	140,000	70,000			70,000	280,000
1972/73	160,000	130,000		422,500	422,500	1,135,000
1973/74	120,000	60,000			621,000	801,000
1974/75	170,000	85,000		618,000	670,000	1,543,000
1975/76	197,500	112,500	247,500		585,000	1,142,500
1976/77	200,000	300,000	765,000			1,265,000
1977/78	370,000	1,909,800	400,000			2,679,800
1978	205,000	1,905,000				2,110,000
1979	710,000	3,750,000	910,000			5,370,000
1980	3,370,000	5,366,000	700,000			9,436,000
1981	7,650,000		2,950,000			10,600,000
1982	8,110,000		2,450,000			10,560,000
1983	10,362,500		2,820,500			13,183,000
1984	12,100,000		2,650,000			14,750,000
1985	12,945,000		2,855,000			15,800,000
1986	18,082,250		2,351,000			20,433,250
1987	17,005,844		3,225,125			20,230,969
1988	16,434,300		4,730,700			21,165,000
1989	18,257,000		5,733,000			23,990,000
1990	25,157,500					25,157,500
1991	19,460,000					19,460,000
1992	14,625,000					14,625,000
1993	10,812,000					10,812,000
Total	196,943,144	13,778,425	32,787,825	1,040,500	2,433,625	246,983,519

Table 3. Danish official support from the Apartheid Appropriation via WUS-Denmark (DKK)

	South Africa	Zimbabwe	Namibia	Angola	Mozambique	Total
1964/65						0
1965/66	61,896					61,896
1966/67	100,000					100,000
1967/68	70,000	70,000				140,000
1968/69	150,500	150,500				301,000
1969/70	200,000	200,000				400,000
1970/71	262,500	262,500				525,000
1971/72	318,000	303,000		50,000		671,000
1972/73	157,000	52,000		1,275,520		1,484,520
1973/74	618,000	342,000		2,914,400		3,874,400
1974/75	920,500	448,500		1,825,000		3,194,000
1975/76	918,125	778,125		1,771,000		3,467,250
1976/77	1,186,500	1,186,500	415,750			2,788,750
1977/78	1,147,000	1,147,000	933,000			3,227,000
1978	1,107,125	1,107,125	803,500			3,017,750
1979	1,235,000	1,235,000	2,615,000			5,085,000
1980	2,490,000	2,290,000	4,500,000			9,280,000
1981	4,760,000		5,940,000			10,700,000
1982	5,100,000		5,750,000			10,850,000
1983	5,520,000		7,460,000			12,980,000
1984	6,920,000		8,360,000			15,280,000
1985	7,250,000		10,000,000			17,250,000
1986	5,520,000		9,365,000			14,885,000
1987	4,840,000		12,660,000			17,500,000
1988	5,400,000		14,170,000			19,570,000
1989	5,625,000		13,625,000			19,250,000
1990	16677932					16,677,932
1991	28,249,394					28,249,394
1992	30,925,255					30,925,255
1993	20,000,000					20,000,000
Total	157,729,727	9,572,250	96,597,250	7,835,920	0	271,735,147

Table 4. Danish official support[1] from the Apartheid Appropriation via DAF / IDAF and IUEF (DKK)

	DAF/IDAF[1]		IUEF
	[1]	[2]	
1964/65			200,000
1965/66	100,096		250,000
1966/67	100,000		350,000
1967/68	105,000		475,000
1968/69	213,000		75,000
1969/70	341,500		770,500
1970/71	229,500		863,000
1971/72	550,000		1,090,000
1972/73	1,650,000		1,160,000
1973/74	1,163,600		1,374,000
1974/75			2,588,000
1975/76	1,300,000		2,523,500
1976/77	2,500,000		3,675,500
1977/78	1,000,000		3,883,000
1978	1,900,000		3,927,500
1979	2,100,000		6,755,000
1980	2,500,000		
1981	2,700,000		
1982	2,600,000		
1983	3,000,000		
1984	2,400,000		
1985	2,400,000		
1986	4,420,000		
1987	5,500,000		
1988	6,000,000		
1989	7,500,000		
1990	7,500,000		
1991	5,600,000	1,200,000	
1992		2,000,000	
1993		1,300,000	
Total	65,372,696	4,500,000	29,960,000

[1] DAF (Defence and Aid Fund), soon becoming IDAF (International Defence and Aid Fund), supported legal aid, humanitarian assistance and education to prisoners and their families inside Southern Africa (1) and in the 1990s university bursaries (2). IUEF (International University Exchange Fund) provided bursaries to exiles until infiltrated by South African intelligence.

Table 5. Danish official support from the Apartheid Appropriation via Danish Refugee Council (DKK)

	Exile bursaries in Swaziland	Mozambique Institute and Am. Boavista Hospital*	*Repatriation Zimbabwe	Total
1964/65				0
1965/66	54,159			54,159
1966/67	55,000	430,000		485,000
1967/68	78,000			78,000
1968/69	65,000			65,000
1969/70	65,000			65,000
1970/71	135,000	500,000		635,000
1971/72	215,000	642,000		857,000
1972/73	226,200	600,000		826,200
1973/74		1,300,000		1,300,000
1974/75		1,500,000		1,500,000
1975/76		1,500,000		1,500,000
1976/77				
1977/78				
1978				
1979				
1980			5,000,000	5,000,000
1981				
1982				
1983				
1984				
1985				
1986				
1987				
1988				
1989				
1990				
1991				
1992				
1993				
Total	893,359	6,472,000	5,000,000	12,365,359

* = in collaboration with UNHCR.

Table 6. Danish official support from the Apartheid Appropriation via UN Trust Funds (DKK)

	Trust Fund for South Africa	Educational and Training Programme for South(/ern) Africa	Nambia Institute and UN Fund for Nambia	Total
1964/65				
1965/66		250000		250,000
1966/67	200,000	550,000		750,000
1967/68	300,000	550,000		850,000
1968/69	400,000			400,000
1969/70	400,000	600,000		1,000,000
1970/71	450,000	700,000		1,150,000
1971/72	500,000	750,000		1,250,000
1972/73	550,000	800,000		1,350,000
1973/74	600,000	850,000		1,450,000
1974/75	650,000	900,000	200,000	1,750,000
1975/76	670,000	920,000	200,000	1,790,000
1976/77	750,000	1,000,000	700,000	2,450,000
1977/78	780,000	1,040,000	800,000	2,620,000
1978	820,000	1,100,000	900,000	2,820,000
1979	1,400,000	1,800,000	1,500,000	4,700,000
1980	1,600,000	2,500,000	1,700,000	5,800,000
1981	2,000,000	3,000,000	2,500,000	7,500,000
1982	2,500,000	3,000,000	3,000,000	8,500,000
1983	2,500,000	3,000,000	4,627,000	10,127,000
1984	2,500,000	3,000,000	5,535,000	11,035,000
1985	3,000,000	3,500,000	7,500,000	14,000,000
1986	3,500,000	4,100,000	8,900,000	16,500,000
1987	4,000,000	4,300,000	9,900,000	18,200,000
1988	4,700,000	4,300,000	10,300,000	19,300,000
1989	5,200,000	4,750,000	11,100,000	21,050,000
1990	4,400,000	4,000,000	6,300,000	14,700,000
1991	3,500,000	3,500,000		7,000,000
1992	2,000,000	2,000,000		4,000,000
1993	1,000,000	1,000,000		2,000,000
Total	50,870,000	57,760,000	75,662,000	184,292,000

Table 7. Danish official support from the Apartheid Appropriation via various transition and democratisation organisations in South Africa (DKK)

	1990	1991	1992	1993	Total
Union of Occupational Therapists: – Bursaires	58,500		51,124		109,624
Danish Centre for Human Rights and Mellemfolkeligt Samvirke: – Human rights and legal aid organisations	354,165	1,475,452	2,358,984	2,234,000	6,422,601
Danish Embassy: –To South African NGOs		198,916	800,000	3,000,000	3,998,916
Lawyers for Human Rights			10,000,000		10,000,000
Danish Council of Organisations of Disabled People: – Support to 'Disabled Peoples International', South Africa			651,630	1,000,000	1,651,630
Various violence monitoring, voter education, police training etc. in South Africa				32,000,000	32,000,000
Danish Union of Journalists: – Training of black journalists, South Africa				465,000	465,000

Table 8. Other allocations from the Apartheid Appropriation (DKK)

Via:	Budget year(s):	Total
Organisation of African Unity		
– Conference in Oslo, 1973	1972/73	100,000
– Health and Education for Liberation Movements:	1974/75	400,000
Angola Committee, Holland: 'Facts and Reports':	1972/73	25,000
Zambia Red Cross: Refugees from South Africa:	1965/66	33,849
PAIGC: Shoes and clothes for children:	1972/73	195,200
'Anti-Imperialist Solidarity':		
– Transport of 2nd hand clothes to MPLA and Frelimo:	1973/74	5,000
Africa National Conference—Zimbabwe:		
– Health, education and agriculture:	1974/75–1975/76	650,000
Luthuli Memorial Foundation:		
– Health Centre, Tanzania:	1976/77	50,000
International Peace Centre for Namibia:	1976/77	75,750
International Liga for Peace and Freedom:		
– Poultry and irrigation project in South Africa:	1976/77–1978	125,000
Africa Educational Trust:		
– Bursaries for South African and Namibian students:	1981–1993	29,143,281
ASF (Danish People's Aid)		
– Kurasini Hospital, Tanzania:	1982	640,000
– Health Clinic, Dakawa:	1983	240,000
– Training Clinic for South African refugees in Angola:	1988	1 285,000
Via SIDA: Nordic Health and Education Programme for SWAPO, Loudima Angola:	1982	2 800,000
Women and Apartheid Conference, Belgium:	1982	50,000
Danish Union of Teachers:		
– Support to South African union of Teachers ATASA:	1986	330,000
DDGU * Youth Sports Projects:	1989	367,500
Lincoln Trust Fund:		
– Bursaries for South Africans in Britain:	1990–1993	1,730,000

Table 9. Danish official support

| | | OF TOTAL | | | | | |
	Total	to South Africa	to Zimbabwe	to Namibia	to Angola	to Mozambique	to Guinea-Bissau	Projects with NMLs[1]
1964/65	200,000	40,000	40,000	40,000	40,000	50,000		
1965/66	750,000	550,000	50,000	50,000	50,000	50,000		
1966/67	1,830,000	1,120,000	70,000	70,000	70,000	70,000		
1967/68	1,690,000	1,260,000	160,000	90,000	90,000	90,000		430,000
1968/69	1,161,000	824,500	336,500					
1969/70	2,650,000	1,702,250	539,500	130,000	130,000	148,250		1,161,000
1970/71	3,600,000	1,437,000	893,625	432,500	145,000	691,875		500,000
1971/72	4,708,000	1,893,000	1,280,500	472,500	200,000	862,000		692,000
1972/73	9,025,920	2,403,000	1,704,500	517,500	1,903,020	1,202,500	1,295,200	4,015,720
1973/74	9,984,000	2,447,800	1,458,400	881,400	3,086,900	2,093,500	16,000	4,791,400
1974/75	12,400,000	2,859,500	1,543,000	1,184,500	3,093,000	2,820,000	900,000	6,353,000
1975/76	12,598,250	3,902,375	2,954,000	1,885,875	1,771,000	2,085,000		3,050,000
1976/77	13,400,000	5,491,750	3,781,000	4,126,625				100,000
1977/78	14,109,800	4,971,000	4,903,800	4,235,000				1,040,000
1978	14,900,000	5,332,875	5,144,875	4,424,250				1,100,000
1979	25,000,000	7,242,500	9,012,500	8,745,000				3,260,000
1980	35,000,000	10,790,000	15,385,000	8,825,000				5,300,000
1981	35,000,000	20,960,000		14,040,000				6,600,000
1982	40,000,000	23,125,000		16,875,000				10,810,000
1983	45,000,000	27,072,500		17,927,500				10,900,000
1984	50,000,000	30,770,000		19,230,000				12,200,000
1985	55,000,000	31,545,000		23,455,000				14,900,000
1986	65,000,000	40,066,250		24,933,750				12,562,800
1987	72,000,000	41,114,875		30,885,125				18,273,969
1988	79,000,000	44,261,800		34,738,200				14,535,000
1989	87,000,000	50,179,000		36,820,500				6,625,000
1990	81,000,000	74,800,000		6,300,000				
1991	78,538,824	78,538,824						10,062,855
1992	81,434,750	81,434,750						12,000,000
1993	81,626,000	81,626,000						12,000,000
Total	679,762,249	49,255,825	261,315,225	10,578,920	10,153,125	2,211,200	172,065,744	1,013,706,544

[1]NMLs = National liberation movements

Table 10. Danish official support divided by sources (DKK)

	Apartheid Appropriation	Multi- and bilateral development assistance funds (Danida)
1964/65		200,000
1965/66	250,000	500,000
1966/67	300,000	1,530,000
1967/68	390,000	1,300,000
1968/69	500,000	661,000
1969/70	600,000	2,050,000
1970/71	700,000	2,900,000
1971/72	1,460,000	3,248,000
1972/73	6,495,720	2,530,200
1973/74	8,450,000	153,400
1974/75	12,400,000	
1975/76	12,598,250	
1976/77	13,400,000	
1977/78	14,109,800	
1978	14,900,000	
1979	25,000,000	
1980	35,000,000	
1981	35,000,000	
1982	40,000,000	
1983	45,000,000	
1984	50,000,000	
1985	55,000,000	
1986	65,000,000	
1987	72,000,000	
1988	79,000,000	
1989	87,000,000	
1990	81,100,000	
1991	78,538,824	
1992	81,434,750	
1993	81,626,000	
Total	997,253,344	16,453,200

Name Index

Abelin, Stig 72
Amathila, Ben 17, 86–87
Andersen, K. B. 16, 31, 41, 43–44, 47–49, 53,
    55–77, 79–83, 86–88, 91–96, 101–103,
    106, 124–125
Andreassen, Knut 53
Basson, Japie 64

Baunsgaard, Hilmar 131
Biko, Steve 99, 104, 118, 121
Boesak, Allan 113
Botha, P. W. 111–112
Budtz, Lasse 87

Cappelen, Andreas 46
Christensen, Steen 59
Christophersen, Henning 106–107
Collins, John 21, 31–32

Dhlamini, Zenani 112
Diallo, Telli 48, 53 65

Elleman-Jensen, Uffe 109, 117, 119

First, Ruth 52–53, 105

Græsholt, Torkild 85
Guldberg, Ove 79–84, 87–97, 106

Hækkerup, Per 23, 26–27, 33, 35, 42, 45, 80
Hartling, Poul 39, 41, 47, 67–70, 75, 79, 83,
    94, 106
Helander, Gunnar 31–32
Hishongwa, Hadino 105
Holt, Karl-Johan 71
Honoré, Bent 88, 93–94

Jensen, Ove 86
Jørgensen, Anker 105, 131

Kampmann, Viggo 20, 23
Kaunda, Kenneth 63, 77
King, Martin Luther 23
Kissinger, Henry 58
Kjeldgaard, Henning 26
Krag, Jens Otto 19, 23–24, 53, 56, 67
Kruse, Max 83, 85–86, 104–105, 109

Langhoff, Johannes 93–94
Lara, Lùcio 51, 54
Larsen, Aksel 24
Lindholt, Holger 88–89, 92
Lissner, Jørgen 85
Luthuli, Albert 23, 33

Mabuza, Lindiwe 17, 20, 112
Maleka, Florence 112
Mandela, Nelson 26–28, 33, 113
Mandela, Winnie 112
Mattsson, Börje 51
McBride, Sean 87
van der Merwe, Paul 64
Minty, Abdul 24, 52, 105, 107
Mondlane, Janet 63, 64
Muller, Hilgard 32
Munk-Plum, Niels 36, 47
Myrdal, Alva 27–29

Nathan, Ove 112
Neto, Agostinho 58, 59, 71–74, 78, 95–96
Nilsson, Torsten 47
Nyerere, Julius 59, 77

Olesen, Kjeld 20, 21, 59, 108, 119
Owen, David 101–102

Petersen, Kristen Helveg 43
Petersen, Niels Helveg 131
Potter, Philip 85

Rasmussen, Hans 66–67
Rasmussen, Poul Nyrup 131
Roberto, Holden 78, 79

Schlüter, Poul 131
Schoon, Marius 112
Sidelmann, Peder 50, 54–55, 57, 71–72, 75,
    83, 88–89, 91–93
Sjollema, Baldwin 84
Stoltenberg, Thorvald 48
Suzman, Helen 112

Tabor, Hans 131
Tambo, Oliver 19–21, 23, 33, 59, 95, 105
Tutu, Desmond 109, 115

Undén, Östen 23

Vestergaard, Leif 84, 85
de Villiers, Graaff 64
Vorster, John 64, 86, 87, 101

Wickman, Krister 48
Winter, Colin 84
Woods, Donald 112
Wulff, Klaus 50, 55, 70, 74, 93–94
Wästberg, Per 59, 112

www.ingramcontent.com/pod-product-compliance
Lightning Source LLC
Chambersburg PA
CBHW081400270326
4193CCB00015B/3369